Brothers in Blue

By

Donald F. Herlihy

authorHOUSE™

1663 LIBERTY DRIVE, SUITE 200
BLOOMINGTON, INDIANA 47403
(800) 839-8640
WWW.AUTHORHOUSE.COM

First published by AuthorHouse 01/05/05

ISBN: 1-4208-0384-0 (sc)

Printed in the United States of America
Bloomington, Indiana

This book is printed on acid-free paper.

THIS BOOK IS DEDICATED TO

AND IN MEMORY OF

MAMA

MY MOTHER

MY MENTOR

MY FRIEND

I WOULD LIKE TO ACKNOWLEDGE

MY WIFE, CONNIE,

WITHOUT HER PERSISTENT

ENCOURAGEMENT

THIS BOOK WOULD NOT HAVE

BEEN WRITTEN.

ALSO TO MY DAUGHTER-IN-LAW, CAROL,

WHO HELPED ME DOT MY I'S AND

CROSS MY T'S.

I LOVE YOU

AND

THANK YOU

BOTH!

TABLE OF CONTENTS

CHAPTER ONE 1

CHAPTER TWO 7

CHAPTER THREE.. 20

CHAPTER FOUR.. 25

CHAPTER FIVE 31

CHAPTER SIX... 36

CHAPTER SEVEN 43

CHAPTER EIGHT 47

CHAPTER NINE.. 53

CHAPTER TEN.. 58

CHAPTER ELEVEN 62

CHAPTER TWELVE 68

CHAPTER THIRTEEN... 72

CHAPTER FOURTEEN 79

CHAPTER FIFTEEN.. 85

CHAPTER SIXTEEN.. 90

CHAPTER SEVENTEEN... 96

CHAPTER EIGHTEEN 103

CHAPTER NINETEEN... 109

CHAPTER TWENTY 115

CHAPTER TWENTY-ONE... 123

CHAPTER TWENTY-TWO 129

CHAPTER TWENTY-THREE 135

CHAPTER TWENTY-FOUR 142

CHAPTER TWENTY-FIVE 147

CHAPTER TWENTY-SIX 151

CHAPTER TWENTY-SEVEN 158

CHAPTER ONE

I was going to be eighteen years of age soon. I attended Bayside High School, where I would have to pass every one of my subjects in order to acquire the thirty-two credits needed to graduate. However, Mrs. Harkins, my English teacher, made sure that graduation would not be something I achieved. I failed Mrs. Harkins' English class, not realizing how that would change the course of my life. Unbeknownst to me, destiny was taking over my life. I had to go home and explain to Mama why there wasn't going to be a graduation, even though I knew this would break my mama's heart.

"Why, Donald? Why? Your brother Billy graduated; your sister Alice is preparing to graduate. Why can't you? Oh Donald! You are always the black sheep of the family. Your father will be furious!"

Billy, who is ten years older than me, had fought in World War II. Billy had come home to a "Hero's Welcome," a party thrown by his family and friends. The devastating part of Billy's homecoming was that he returned home blind. His sight had been taken from him by a German tank shell in the invasion of Normandy. It took years before my brother gave me the details of the events that lead up to losing his sight.

During the war, Billy and another young soldier were on the road when a German tank appeared ahead of them. Billy picked up his bazooka, positioned it on his shoulder, and told the young GI to load it with a bazooka shell. The young GI followed his orders, and Billy sighted in on the tank, and then his finger pulled the trigger mechanism. At the same time, the German soldier in the tank pulled the trigger on his cannon. The German tank shell exploded about ten feet in front of Billy and blew him off the ground twenty-five feet into a gully, knocking him unconscious. Billy had no idea how long he had been knocked out, but when he woke a medic was bandaging his eyes. Billy turned to the medic and asked, "Where is the young soldier who was with me?"

The medic told him that he was up on the road—dead. Billy could not understand how this could happen since the shell exploded in front of him, and the young soldier was behind Billy. "Why him?" Billy asked. "Why him and not me?"

Suddenly, the medic dragged Billy into a large storm drain and told him to keep very quiet. The Germans had overrun their position and Germans were everywhere. He gave Billy a shot of morphine for the pain and told him he would be back soon.

The medic returned with another wounded soldier who was loudly crying in pain. The medic told Billy that he only had one shot of morphine left. Billy said, "Give him the shot, or we will all die." Hours later, the Germans had left the area, and the American forces were now able to pick up their wounded. My brother Billy was, of course, among them. Soon, Billy was homeward bound decorated with the Silver and Bronze Star with clusters, along with a Purple Heart.

So, it wasn't that I had to follow in Billy's footsteps, but it did put a lot of pressure on me. School, graduation—what would I become in this world? Did Mama expect me to match up to Billy's feats? That would be impossible, and I knew it. I would pray every night—not to be better than my brother, but to at least make my mama proud of me. I told my mama that I would attend night school to get my diploma. I knew darn well that I had no intention of doing anything of the sort.

Instead, I hooked up with my lifelong friends, Stewie Norman and Jerry Beckerman, in what was called Windsor Park. There, hidden away in a little nook of Union Turnpike was a cocktail bar known as The Black Rose. This became our meeting place and watering hole for months to come.

As time passed, we would do our beer drinking in the Rose and wait for a call from Stewie's service. Stewie had bought a cigarette vending machine, a bowling machine, and a jukebox, which were located in various areas of Queens. When his service would notify him that a machine was broken, all three of us would go to the location. Naturally, Jerry and I would look on as Stewie proceeded to fix the machine. When all was done, it was back to the Black Rose for a couple of cold ones and to meet the girls: Lynn, Irene, and Roberta.

After several months had passed, I decided to join the army. There was one problem—Mama would hit the roof. She had given the eyes of one son to her country, and she was not going to allow another one to step in harm's way. At this time, the Korean War was at its peak. I knew it was only a matter of months before I would be drafted, and the waiting around was pure hell. There were no jobs available to young men of draft age. Employers didn't want to risk training these men only to lose them to the draft.

The "Three Musketeers," as we called ourselves, would have to meet in the Rose and figure a way to pull this off without Mama getting upset. There was a fear that Mama would write to President Truman; in which case, the poor man would get a taste of Mama's wrath. Soon, we solved the problem. I would go down to the draft board and request my draft notice be pushed to the top of the list. The following week, the white business-like envelope appeared on the kitchen table. Mama just stared at it and the title of the return address: Selective Service Department.

I opened it in front of her and acted surprised. Mama looked at me and said, "Why are you surprised?" I stood there thinking, how could she possibly know that I pushed up my draft notice? Mama turned and said, "Now you see what happens when you quit high school. What do you have to say for yourself now?" I felt such relief knowing that my scheme was not discovered. Even though Mama would not write President Truman, she was not very happy to be sending another son off to war.

The following week I was sent to Fort Dix, New Jersey, for basic training, which would last eight weeks. While at Fort Dix, I met this southern boy from Georgia, Charlie Giddens, and we hit it off. Charlie had an infectious laugh, so if you were anywhere near Charlie when he was laughing, you would find yourself laughing too and not even know why. That was Charlie! During the fourth or fifth week of basic training, Charlie and I were getting homesick for New York City and a couple of cold beers. Weekend passes were given out to the other soldiers, but Charlie and I had pulled fire watch and were not able to leave the camp.

It was our duty to make sure that the coal furnaces in four of the barracks had a nice supply of coal and tempered flame. Charlie, however, had an idea. This idea would later cause us heartaches beyond our wildest nightmares. Charlie suggested that we put enough coal in the furnaces to keep them going for five or six hours while we went to New York. We figured we would be back before dawn and we would still have plenty of time to stand reveille. No one would miss us. The one thing that Charlie didn't know was that furnaces have to be stoked— the coals have to be moved around every so often or the fires will go out, and go out they did. The sergeant major was notified around three in the morning and we were declared awol at three ten that same morning.

We were in the chow line, waiting for breakfast after a beautiful night of drinking and carousing in New York City. We were laughing and oh-so-proud that we had pulled our plan off without a hitch, when two military policemen approached and informed us that we were under arrest for being awol. We were escorted to the sergeant major's office.

The sergeant major was a tall man standing about six-foot-three inches, with a chest full of combat medals. He immediately informed us that we would be courts-martialed under military law for being absent without leave. In military law, there are three types of courts-martial: a summary court-martial (this one the lesser of the three), a special court-martial, and a general court-martial (this one can get you shot by a firing squad and we knew this one did not apply—or did it?). We were both starting to get the picture that we didn't know as much about life as we thought we did. We did know, however, that we could only be charged with the lesser of the three, which was a summary court-martial.

While standing at attention in front of the sergeant major, I leaned over to Charlie and whispered, "A fine mess you got us into this time, Ollie!" Then it happened. Charlie started to laugh and it was a boisterous laugh, which of course, made me start to laugh. The only one not laughing was the sergeant major. He looked both of us right in the eye and said, "You will both be charged with a special court-martial." The laughter came to an abrupt halt as we were escorted by military police to the base stockade.

A few days later Charlie and I were again escorted to the building where the courts-martial proceedings would be held. As I stood in front of the four officers who were going to hear the case, I thought to myself, Mama" was right, I am the black sheep of the family and Mama will not be proud of me now. We entered a guilty plea to the charges that day. I was sentenced to ten days in the stockade doing hard labor, and a forfeiture of two months pay. Charlie also forfeited two months pay and he was transferred to another base. Charlie was transferred to Georgia, which was a short distance from his home. This is punishment? Charlie was laughing uncontrollably outside the building, but this time Charlie was the only one laughing.

Ten days went by and I was released from the stockade. I was waiting orders to be shipped out, to God only knows where, and the barracks I was billeted in were empty because my company had already shipped out while I was in the stockade. There was, however, one soldier who was in the stockade with me awaiting for orders. The soldier looked as though he was carrying the world on his back. I asked him if anything was wrong. The soldier told me that he was waiting for a hardship discharge because he was the sole support of his ill mother. He said if he didn't get out of the army, there would be no way his mother could survive. The army was aware of this, but he had to wait for his orders to be cut before he would be released.

He looked and spoke in a laid-back manner, as though he had worked on a farm all his life. All I knew was that I felt sorry for him. The following day, the orders were delivered to us. My orders read that I would spend the duration of my tour at Fort Dix. The farm boy was being sent to Korea.

As I read his orders, I felt so sad for this farm boy, who at this point was in tears. I felt that if I stayed at Fort Dix, it would only be more trouble for me. It occurred to me that maybe I could do something good for this farm boy. At the very least, for the first time in my life I would be doing something, shall we say, noble? Mama had never found out that I pushed up the draft, and there would be no need for her to know that I was going to switch orders with the farm boy, go to Korea, and as Mama would say—put myself in harm's way.

The switching of orders had to be approved by the adjutant general. The adjutant general is there to help any soldier with a problem. We both went before the adjutant general and explained our request. The general looked at me and asked, "How much money is this soldier paying you to go to Korea in his place?" I couldn't believe what I had just heard because that thought had never entered my mind. I told the general the story about my brother serving in World War II, and that I would also like to fight for my country. The general liked my last phrase and approved my request. Two days later, I was flown to Seattle, Washington, and put on the U.S.S. General John J. Pope, a troop carrier headed for Inchon, Korea.

CHAPTER TWO

Mama always said, "Be careful what you wish for; you may just get your wish." This is how I ended up in Korea, a country that seemed as though even God had forgotten it. Korea was brutally cold and desolate with endless snow-covered mountains and valleys. A barren country where 40,000 U.S. soldiers would be killed and 400,000 North Koreans would give up their lives in mortal combat during the war.

Now, I was on the U.S.S. General John J. Pope headed for Inchon, Korea. This journey would take about seventeen days. But, the ship was out to sea for only one day, when seasickness struck me, and the seasickness continued for the next fifteen days. I spent most of those days on the upper deck heaving over the side, when I could get there. Otherwise, I threw-up where I sat on the ship, pleading with anyone walking by to throw me overboard. I figured I would die in Korea anyway, so why not now?

The ship hit a storm about halfway across the ocean. No one was prepared for the fury that the ocean was about to unleash on us. Waves were ten to fifteen feet high. The bow of the ship would go up in the air, at least twenty-five feet high, and then come down with a thunderous thud. I felt my stomach go to my ankles. The bow would disappear underwater and then reappear. This happened over and over again. The storm lasted one full day and night. I huddled below deck in the forward latrine, squatting on the floor with my head well into the toilet bowl. My thoughts were those of a child, are we there yet?

The day finally arrived. The ship landed in the Port of Inchon in the Yellow Sea. All the soldiers began to disembark. And, my feet were finally planted on good ole terra firma, but it took a long time for my knees to stop shaking. We were loaded on to duce and a half trailers, which were better known as "cattle cars." We started the journey to—where? No one knew except the driver and the sergeant. When we asked, "Where are we going?"

The reply was "you'll know when we get there!"

The long ride took us through Yongdungpo, Seoul and north to Wejongbu, just short of what was later known as the 38th parallel. This was to be home. It didn't take long for me to fit in with the other GIs. It took even less time to enter my new life of manhood. Although I would spend my nineteenth birthday in Korea, I think my life as a man started the minute I boarded the ship in Seattle. I had resigned myself to the fact that if I didn't get killed in this God-forsaken country, I would never return to the United States on another ship. I would welcome death rather than be seasick again for another two weeks. I would rather stay in Korea, marry some gook, and live my life in a hooch, then get back on a ship. As quickly as that thought entered by mind, I got it out of my mind. I had confidence in myself to believe that I would think of something, if and when the time ever came that I would get to go home.

Soon, after getting acquainted with my surroundings, a sergeant told me that I would be better off if I got rid of the M1 rifle that weighed nine pounds. He issued me a Carbine, which was a much lighter weapon. He said the M1 clip carried eight rounds and was accurate up to five hundred yards. The Carbine, on the other hand, could carry a clip of thirty rounds. When taped upside down to another clip, it could give me firepower of up to sixty rounds. The first sergeant informed me that in a combat condition, if the North Koreans overran our position, we would only have between ten to one hundred feet from the onslaught of a gook attack.

Dick Butler, from Troy, New York, was the first soldier who introduced himself to me. He showed me how to dress in my sheepskin-lined parker. He also told me of the useless items in my mess kit that I could throw away. He told me I should only keep the spoon from my mess kit. He said the knife and fork would clang together alerting the gooks to my position. They are known to pick up on that in a New York minute. Dick's words of wisdom were "keep the spoon in a separate pocket and above all, try to stay dry. If your Mickey Mouse boots feel as though you're in water; it's because they are. You must empty out the water because otherwise your feet will sweat. Keep extra socks on you because you don't want your feet to get frostbitten."

I am now saying to myself, how the hell am I going to get through eighteen months over here? since a soldier must do a year and a half before rotating home. Months had passed, and I always looked forward to getting mail from home. Mama wrote at least twice a week. She would always put a few packages of Kool-Aid in the envelope for the guys and me to enjoy. In one of her letters, she told me that Stewie and Jerry went down to the Army Recruiting Center to enlist. Stewie was rejected for some medical reason associated with his feet but Jerry was accepted. This brought a smile to my face. Jerry could never make up his mind about anything we wanted to do, where we should do it, what time we should do it, and so forth. We gave him the nickname "Shoulda Coulda Woulda" and that name fit him perfectly. I couldn't help thinking that he was probably now saying, "I should have stayed home; I would have stayed home; and I could have stayed home. Why the hell didn't I stay home?" That was Jerry Beckerman.

A few days after receiving Mama's letter, Butler and I were returning from a patrol. Butler decided to take a short cut back to the compound. This entailed crossing the Hahn River at a narrow point. The river was frozen, as was everything else. I told Butler that I had my doubts about the thickness of the ice. I wasn't too confident that it would hold our weight. Butler disregarded my concern and said, "No problem. We can save a couple of miles this way."

We were about two hundred feet from shore, and Butler was leading, when I started to see water appear where he was stepped. I stopped in my tracks, and yelled for Butler to stop! But it was too late. First his right foot went through the ice up to his knee, and then his left foot broke through the ice. Then, his whole body disappeared below the ice. Everything seemed like it was taking place in slow motion. I stood there in complete and absolute shock, as well as panic. Then, pushing up and out of the water, like The Creature from the Black Lagoon, appeared Butler. I will never forget the look on his face. He was drowning. He yelled, "Help! Help me!"

I stood there telling myself to turn my feet around and run back to the safety of the shore. No one would have to know the truth. He would just be another casualty of war. I only stood there for a second or two, but it seemed like minutes had gone by as I watched him. I knew in my heart, if I tried to save Butler, this would be the place I would die.

I edged myself close to the three foot opening where Butler was frantically grabbing the ice to stay afloat. Not thinking clearly, I took off my glove and told Butler to grab the glove, and not my hand. I should have used my Carbine with a sling to give him something stronger to grab.

Butler leaped forward, and put a death grip around my wrist pulling me over his head, launching me on a forty-five degree angle into the frigid water. I did not expect to be pulled into the river so I had not taken a deep breath of air. My rifle came off my shoulder as I entered the water on a downward plunge. I immediately began to swim up to the surface. My lungs were bursting for air. My head struck the solid ice, and I was nowhere near the hole where Butler had pulled me into the water. I was now under the ice and at a complete loss for any sense of direction.

My arms were moving in every direction. I couldn't see a thing. The water had become cloudy because Butler had churned up so much sediment in his effort to stay afloat. My sheepskin-lined fatigue jacket and my pants were sucking up the water and weighing me down. I thought, Oh God! What a way to die!

All of a sudden, I felt something kick me in the back. I turned in the water and grabbed at it, not knowing what it was that I felt. It was Butler's legs. I held onto his legs and pulled him down so that I could get to the hole that he made in the ice. I broke through the surface and filled my lungs with that, oh-so-precious, air. No sooner had I taken that breath of air, then Butler grabbed my waist and pulled me under the water again. This time he stood on my shoulders as he attempted to pull himself up and onto the ice. Not a good idea on Butler's part as it simply pushed me deeper into the water. I broke free from his legs and surfaced again, and as I surfaced I started swinging my fists at him. I connected squarely with his face. I yelled at him, "Calm down! Calm down or we're both going to drown!" Butler looked at me like a wounded puppy and began to back off and calm down.

We both started to tread water. I looked up at the hillside and saw Korean soldiers in the distance watching us. If they were North Koreans, they would soon be taking pot shots at us while we were helpless in the water. We both kept our eyes on the hill, and there were no sounds of gunfire, so we assumed they were ROK (Republic of Korea) soldiers who were on our side.

The air temperature was around fifteen degrees, and the water temperature had to be below zero. I told Butler that there was no way we would be able to pull ourselves out of the water and onto the ice. We had to break the ice with our elbows as we headed towards shore. We were side by side in the water and facing the shore. In order to keep afloat, we would kick our feet and reach our elbows high and come down on the ice with as much force as we could muster. The ice would break and slowly drift behind us. We had now been in the frigid water for about forty-five minutes and our faces were numb.

It would only be a matter of time before hypothermia would set in and our brain functioning would begin to decline. We kept breaking ice and moving towards the shore a few feet at a time. We were about twenty feet off shore when we hit ice that was four to five inches thick. It wouldn't break! As many times as we hit the ice, it just refused to give way.

I was completely exhausted, and I did not have an ounce of strength left in me. There was just no sense to it. I committed myself to the water. I lay back, as I started going under the water, and said a prayer. The last thing I saw was Butler coming down on the ice with his bare knuckles. The water turning red from his blood. The heavy block of ice in front of me disappeared under the water, as I slipped beneath the surface for the last time, peace and serenity at last.

Suddenly, I found myself coughing up a lot of the river, and when I opened my eyes I saw that I was on the bank of the river, with Butler kneeling over me. At the very last moment, he had grabbed the collar of my fatigue jacket and floated me to shore. I looked up at him. Not a word was spoken between us. Our eyes said it all. He reached into his jacket and handed my fatigue hat to me. He said, "You will need this." When he had taken ahold of my wrist, pulling me into the ice hole, my hat had come off my head. He had grabbed my hat, while in the water, and put it in his jacket. I looked at him and said, "We were about to drown and you saved my hat!"

We crawled up the bank away from the River. It was then that we saw the ROK soldiers. They were speaking to us in Korean. Unknown to me, Butler spoke fluent Korean and was speaking with the soldiers. I was amazed Butler spoke this very difficult language. The soldiers made a large fire, and we sat as close as possible to the warm flames. Steam rose from our wet clothes as we sat there shivering. Butler turned to me and said, "I owe you my life, Don. Whatever money I make in my lifetime, half of it will be yours."

I replied, "You have things backwards; you saved my life."

Butler said, "That's not the way I see it." I thought to myself, what crazy things are said when we encounter a near-death experience.

Hours later, we found our way back to our unit. They asked, "Where the hell were you guys?"

As tired as we were, Butler looked at me and smiled, turned to them and said, "We stopped off at the local pub for a couple of beers."

Within minutes we had crawled into our sleeping bags, and a blissful sleep embraced us.

The devastating winter had finally passed; spring went by in a flash and summer was upon us. This brought the dreaded rainy season. Everywhere we stepped, we were in mud that was ankle deep.

Every day there was a Recon Patrol (Reconnaissance Patrol) sent out, which sought out information about enemy positions or installations. Jim Martin, another GI whom I had met—also from New York, and I had pulled the recon duty that day.

We were sent to the ridge of a mountain, walking along a very narrow path, and about thirty feet down the slope, off to our right, was a cliff with a three hundred foot drop into the canyon. I was walking point when the soft ground beneath me gave way. Immediately, I was on my back and sliding down the treacherous slope. The hill had been leveled in a previous action; therefore, there were no trees or bushes to grab. I thought, Oh God! I'm in trouble again! I slid for ten or twelve feet. My arms stretched out, and my fingers digging into the soil. Then I felt a terrible pain in my balls. I had come to a complete stop. At my crotch was a small pine tree, no more than one foot high and one inch round. I sat upright and could see the edge of the cliff.

I placed the palm of my hands flat on either side of me. I knew if I moved at all, I would definitely fall again and go off the cliff into oblivion. From above, I heard Martin yell, "Don't move! Don't move a muscle!" He took the sling from his rifle, the ammo bandolier that he carried, and his pant's belt, and knotted them together to make a rope. He threw this down to me, and it landed near my right hand. Knowing this was my only lifeline, I moved my right hand to grab the rope. This movement put more weight on the small pine tree, and it started to bend in down. I rolled onto my right side and grabbed the leather sling with both hands. Martin slowly pulled me up the cliff to him. I stood up holding my crotch. I felt like I had been kicked in the balls by a mule.

I thanked Martin. I thought to myself, why couldn't I have been this creative when I was in the predicament with Butler? Soon, I was complaining about this rotten country. Martin shut me up when he said, "You're alive, aren't you! Stop your bitching!"

I looked at him and said, "You're right. Let's get back to the unit."

A few months had passed, and the weather was getting cold again. Butler had received word that he was rotating home. Although I was very happy for Butler it sure did depress me. I knew

I would miss him. When his day arrived we shook hands, and gave each other a hug. Neither one of us said a word. Butler jumped on the truck, and then he was off to a waiting ship that would bring him back to the good old USA and the life of a civilian.

I was becoming what we called a short timer, and I couldn't wait until I would be boarding a ship to go home. Now I was thinking, so what if I get a little seasick? The days were very long after Butler left. I found myself taking long walks, far from the compound. This went against common logic since we were close to the border. Of course, these walks got me in trouble, again. The difference was that I was alone.

I had just entered an area of thick brush, when I heard movement in the bushes. I stopped and listened for a moment when out of the thicket in front of me came a Korean soldier. He wore heavily padded clothing. I looked down at his boots, which were also padded. Only North Koreans wore padded boots. It was then that I realized that I must have crossed over into the Demilitarized Zone (DMZ).

The soldier was carrying a double-barreled shotgun, which struck me as odd, and he was pointing it right at me. I pushed the lever on my Carbine to automatic, and we stood there with weapons leveled at each other. Something on my right shoulder said, "Kill him!" Yet something on my left shoulder said, "No!" If I pulled the trigger, I knew I would hit him with at least fifteen rounds. If he pulled both triggers on his way down, he couldn't miss me with that scattergun. It was then I remembered what the sergeant had said, and realized that we were only ten feet apart.

From behind me, I heard a noise from the direction that I had come. I turned my head slowly to the side. Out of the corner of my eye, I saw another North Korean with a shotgun pointing at my back. I knew one of them was going to shoot me. I found comfort in knowing I was going to take at least one of them with me, preferably, the one standing in front of me. Both of them looked as frightened as I felt right then. They reminded me of the Mexican bandits you would see in a movie. They were short and thin, ragged looking with their bandoliers criss-crossed over their chest, and the bandoliers were filled with shotgun shells.

What puzzled me was that the weapons they were carrying, were not those of a fighting soldier. They started talking to each other in their gibberish language. I thought to myself, why couldn't Butler be here? Just then, the gook that was behind me motioned with his shotgun that I should follow the man in front of me. I knew then that I was being taken prisoner. But I could not understand why they were not taking my weapon from me. We walked very slowly and quietly for about one hundred yards. As we walked, I was trying to sort out what was happening and what was going to be my plan of action, which I didn't have yet.

All of a sudden, the soldier in front of me yelled one word. It was one of the words I knew in Korean that meant "deer." The gook who had been behind me suddenly ran in front of me. I stopped dead in my tracks. Now everything was becoming clearer. These two were probably deserters, as evidenced by their ragged clothes, double-barreled shotguns, leaving me with my weapon, and their interest in deer. They were probably hungry. I did an about face and put my ass in fast gear. I ran south for about fifteen minutes at top speed. Flash Gordon would have had a hard time keeping up with me. When I made it back to the compound, I related the story to a few guys. They all agreed that I was one lucky bastard.

Time passed, and winter was once more upon us, and the holidays were just around the corner. It was my turn according to the roster, to man the outpost position, which was a short distance away. I would be there for the night and be relieved in the morning. I looked forward to the solitude and my thoughts of home.

It was a very dark and quiet moonless night, so if we had to smoke we did it under our poncho. I had settled down quietly in an elongated trench, when I heard a noise approaching my position. I stood up in the trench with my Carbine ready. "Psst. Psst. Herlihy. Herlihy, where are you?"

I quickly pulled him into the trench and said, "Why don't you blow a horn while your at it, asshole?" I asked him what he was doing here. And he asked me if I had a high school diploma. I looked at him startled and said, "You're kidding me, right?"

He replied, "No. You can go back to Seoul, Korea, for a test."

I said, "Get the hell out of here before you get us both killed." The skinny kid crawled out of the trench. I sat there thinking, Holy Shit! "Psst. Psst. Hey kid come back here." He crawled back into the trench. I asked him, "How many days would I be in Seoul?" He told me that I would be taken off the line, and I would take one test a day for five days. "Yes. Yes. Sign me up." I smiled to myself and thought, Mama didn't raise no fool.

A couple of days later, I was in Seoul relaxing and taking the GED tests for my high school diploma. I passed with a mark of eighty-four. The officer in charge asked me if I would like the diploma sent to my home. "Yes, indeed," I answered. I could just picture Mama's face beaming with pride. I knew that would make her day.

On the sixth day, I was back with my unit. I still had a few days off coming to me. Mama had written to me that Bob McCrindle, who lived around the corner from us, was in Korea attached to the 24th Infantry Division in Dog Company. I asked the sergeant if I could have a jeep for a day so I could go see a buddy of mine in the 24th Division. He said everything was quiet so it would be all right as long as I returned by nightfall.

The 24th was a few miles away from us, and I found it without any problems. I asked a few soldiers in Bravo Company where I might find Bobby McCrindle. One guy asked me if I was a good friend of Macs. I said, "Yea, we grew up together in Bayside, New York."

He replied, "Great, I'll take you to him. I have to relieve him, and he is not in the best mood." I asked why and he said, "Mac has been dug in on an outpost hill and hasn't had a shower in three days. He's been taking whores baths out of his helmet and eating "K" rations. I laughed and we introduced ourselves. His name was Howie. He told me that Mac was a great guy. We had to walk slowly up a few hills. Howie said, "You have to be careful. We are very close to minefields."

I said, "You got to be fucking kidding me." It was then that I heard a click and looked down at my foot. Off to the side, I saw the small red triangle sign that designated a minefield. I called to Howie, "I think I'm fucking on one."

Howie turned and came back to me. "Did you hear a loud click?" he asked.

"Yea! Yea! I did. Am I on one?"

He bent down to my left foot, took out his bayonet and stuck it slowly into the ground underneath my boot and said, "Yup, you're on a Betsy!"

A bouncing Betsy is the name of an antipersonnel mine made to maim the soldier. If you step on one and don't hear the click, and you step off, the mine is propelled upwards behind you about two to three feet in the air and then explodes. This will send shrapnel into your legs and body, or it simply will take off the bottom of your leg. It can be disarmed as long as you keep your weight on the mine and someone else puts a carter pin into the mechanism. This is also dangerous, however, because the Koreans are known to attach a second mine below the first one. They call this a "Booby Trap." It will almost certainly kill the soldier who has his face close to the ground, and definitely the one standing on the mine. The North Koreans it as getting two for the price of one.

Howie said, "Just relax."

Oh sure, no problem. I'm standing on dynamite and I should relax. I thought to myself, why does this country want my soul so bad? Howie methodically cleaned the dirt away with his hands. He then went into his pocket and removed a small carter pin, pushing it into the mechanism. Now he had to remove more dirt under the mine looking for a booby trap.

He then stood up, looked at me, and said, "You're clear."

I stood and said, "What the hell does that mean?"

He said, "There's no booby trap, the Betsy's disarmed."

I said, "In your dreams. I can tell by the look on your face that you're not sure."

At that point, he grabbed me by my jacket and pulled me forward off the mine. Howie looked me straight in the eye and said, "I'm sure. We can go now."

We reached the outpost, and there stood Mac with a big smile on his face. He couldn't believe I had found him in this war-torn hellhole. Mac was relieved by Howie, and he was anxious to get back to his company. I wasn't. I explained to Mac what had happened to me on the way up to the outpost. He said, "That happens often. The men in this company are well trained in disarming antipersonnel mines. Just stay behind me on the way down." I asked him if he carried carter pins. His reply, sure do.

On the way down the hill, I couldn't help thinking that I was much better off in my unit compared to where Mac was on the hill. When we got back to Mac's company, we ate chow and then sat around bullshitting about old times. I left Mac a few hours later. I said, "Take care of yourself."

He said, "You do the same."

Thanksgiving, and my second Christmas in this land, had passed without incident. Now, it was February and a very bitter cold day. I heard the sergeant yelling, "Herlihy. Herlihy."

I called out, "Over here, Sarge."

Then I heard him say, "Get your gear together. Your rotating!" I could not believe my ears. It had finally happened. I was leaving this land that was so hell-bent on taking my life. Now, if only the guardian angel that took such good care of me would stay with me for a little while longer, I'd make it back home.

The name of the ship was U.S.S. General Mann. After spending eighteen long months here, the ship was a beautiful sight. When I boarded, I told the officer that I really get a bad case of seasickness. He said, "Fine, you can give out the seasick pills at the entrance to the galley."

The first day out of port, I did great. I handed out the pills and took many of them for myself. The second day began a repeat performance of the trip over to Korea. Only this time, each day brought me closer to home and my family. With this in mind, getting seasick wasn't as bad.

We landed at the Port of San Francisco. We were then trucked to a repo-depo base where we turned in all of our clothes that we wore in Korea. New uniforms and combat boots were issued, and we went through a complete medical check. After a few days and a ton of paperwork, we received orders to report to a new base. My orders were to report to Fort Dix, New Jersey. A thirty day pass was issued to everyone. We also received airline tickets to an airport located close to home.

After all this time of being away from home, I didn't want to call anyone. I wanted my homecoming to be a surprise. And it was a surprise. When Mama and Dad saw me walk into the kitchen with my duffel bag, I thought they were going to have heart attacks. Mama let out a scream that the whole neighborhood could hear. Both of them were crying and hugging me at the same time. Mama took my face in her hands and said, "Thank God! My prayers have been answered, your home."

Dad stared at me and said, "You're not hurt are you? They called where you were a conflict, the Korean Conflict."

I looked at him and said, "A conflict. You could have fooled me!"

This was how I dreamed coming home would be while I was in Korea. When Mama and I were alone, she showed me my GED diploma and said, "You did it, Donald. You did it for your Mama!" I was happy to be home, and very happy that I made Mama proud.

CHAPTER THREE

I was a free man for thirty days. All the things I thought I would do when I returned home, were no longer important. I found myself content just sitting with Mama on the porch and reminiscing. She asked me what I missed the most besides the family and her home cooked meals during my time in the service. I said, "Believe it or not, now I appreciate walking on a cement sidewalk." As weird as that sounded, it was the truth and that made Mama laugh. Mama filled me in on all the dirt as she called it, who had gotten married, who was now divorced, and what neighbors had moved out of Bayside.

Then she turned to me and said, "Donald, I don't want you going to work right away. You should stay home and relax. You've certainly earned it." This was music to my ears. I had Mama's permission to bum around rather than go to work.

I thought about this for a while and decided that Mama was right. All I had to do is report back to the army, after my leave was up, and sign a few papers agreeing to do six years in the Army Reserve. Then I would pick up my mustering out pay and my honorable discharge, and I would be a civilian again. I would now be enrolled in the "fifty-two week club." This was a benefit that entitled honorably discharged soldiers twenty-six dollars a week for a total of fifty-two weeks, compliments of Uncle Sam. That was enough to keep me going until I landed a job.

After a few days, I called Stewie and asked him to meet me at The Black Rose. When I walked into the Rose, Stewie had a cold beer waiting for me. We hugged and looked each other up and down, laughing happily that we were finally together again. The owner of The Black Rose came over to me and shook my hand saying he was glad that I was back home. He had missed my money!

Stewie explained to me how he had expanded his vending business. When I left, he had three locations. Now, he had almost one hundred locations. He had built the business slowly and now the profits from it provided a very lucrative income. The girls, Irene, Lynn and Roberta, arrived, and we all set out to Stewie's sister's house.

Stewie's sister, whose name was also Lynn, and her husband, Sandy, were two of the nicest people you would ever meet. Lynn and Sandy were about ten years older than we were and always in dire need of a babysitter. Stewie would babysit their twin girls. In return, they allowed us to have a small party in their finished basement. They were comfortable with this as long as the twins were looked after and nothing was broken. That night Lynn and Sandy went out on the town, and I had the greatest homecoming ever given to one guy.

Several days later, I went to see Carol Covino. She was the girl I had dated before I enlisted in the army. Her mother answered the door. Seeing me, she got this disgusted look on her face. She informed me that her daughter was out on a date and wouldn't be home until very late. Then, she closed the door in my face. I would learn later that Carol's mother told her that she did not want her to date me. She said I was nothing but a common laborer. Because Carol was a registered nurse, her mother felt her daughter should be dating doctors.

A few months went by and I was becoming bored. I joined the Carpenters Union as an apprentice thinking I might as well be what people thought of me, a common laborer. I worked hard insulating new homes being built on Long Island. The money I made was top scale pay. I would give Mama half of my pay. The rest I kept for carfare and whatever else I might need it for.

I was working steady. I was dating Irene and Carol. In my spare time I would hang out with Stewie. A short time later, Carol suggested that we get engaged. This came as a complete surprise to me. I hadn't been home that long and I really wasn't ready for marriage. I agreed but explained to her that there would not be a wedding for a couple of years. I told Mama that Carol and I were going to get engaged. Mama said, "I want you to buy that girl a nice ring. Here is the money you sent me while you were overseas."

I just looked at her and said, "I sent you that money for you to use to help with the bills. Why didn't you use it?"

Mama smiled and said, "Now just take it, Donald. You've been a good boy for your Mama and Dad." My eyes filled up with tears as we gave each other a big hug.

I did what Mama told me to do. I bought Carol a beautiful ring. But when she tried to show it to her mother, her mother refused to look at it. I told Stewie and Jerry about this incident. Jokingly, I said, "I get the distinct impression that Carol's mother doesn't like me."

The Three Musketeers were together again and enjoying life to the fullest. Jerry had told Stewie that he had invested a few hundred dollars in a company that sold men's shirts. Immediately Stewie and I echoed, "You shoulda, woulda, coulda or you did invest?" Jerry laughed but explained to us that he did make this investment. Little did we know at that time, but Jerry would become one of the top buyers in this line of clothes. His few hundred dollars made him a millionaire, and that's an achievement!

I never imagined that two years would fly by so fast, but it did. Soon, our wedding day was just around the corner. There were many difficult and stressful times during the planning of this wedding. But, I guess it was all worth while because the wedding turned out to be a very nice affair. Carol's mother attended and didn't have that look of disappointment on her face. Our wedding didn't change her hostile feelings towards me and I just put it in my mind that I would not let this woman get the best of me.

It didn't take long for Carol to become pregnant. I was soon to be the proud dad of a little girl named Debbie. One day after work I stopped by Mama's house, as I often did on the way home from work. We sat on the porch, enjoying each other's company. Mama turned to me and said, "Donald, I want you to take the test to become a New York City police officer."

I looked at her and said, "What are you crazy? I hate cops. All they do is break people's chops." As the words came out, I realized that this was no way to speak to Mama. For a split second, I thought Mama was going to get up and get the strap. My sister, Alice, and I had felt the sting of that strap many a time when we were, as Mama would put it, bad.

Mama said, "Please give this some thought. Do it for Mama. You will be the only police officer in the family, and you will be able to retire in twenty years."

I sat there thinking, I'm only twenty-three years old and my mama has me retiring already. Mama just stared at me—hoping and praying. I said, "Mama, if that's what you want, I'll take the next test when it comes up."

Mama immediately said, "There's one in two weeks so go down to the post office and make out the application tomorrow." I laughed to myself and thought, Mama got me again. I took the test and passed. It would be almost two years before the police department would call anyone for the job.

Meanwhile, I had left construction work and landed a job with a company that was installing monorail systems for clothing manufacturers. It was a new concept to the industry and every clothing manufacturer wanted one installed. Most of the manufacturers wanted it done yesterday. I had become a foreman supervisor and I was receiving very good pay for those times. I worked long hours and I frequently had to be in Chicago, Tennessee, and Florida. I was needed in these states to setup and hire a crew to install the system. This work schedule was not conducive to a happy marriage.

I was overseeing a job in Hollywood, Florida, when I received a call from Carol who was now pregnant with our second child a child who would later be named Carolyn. Carol told me that I had received a letter stating that I was accepted into the New York City Police Department. The letter also stated that I had to report on December 27th.

It was three days before Christmas, and I was due to go home anyway. Now I had to make the agonizing decision of either staying with this job or becoming a police officer. I kept seeing the image of Mama's face when I told her I would become a police offer if it would make her happy. And I had made that promise to her.

I went to the boss of the monorail company and told him that I was quitting the job to become a part of the New York City Police Department. He said he was going to make it hard for me to quit. I looked at him not knowing what the hell he was talking about now. He said he knew of the hardship I sustained going out of state so often, and that my wife was unhappy. He was going to raise my salary to two hundred and fifty dollars a week, and I would only be required to go out of state once a year.

Oh my God! What should I do? That was more money than I ever dreamed of making. I ran home and told Carol the company just offered me the deal of a lifetime. She naturally rejected the idea of my staying with them, and claimed she couldn't live this kind of life. I knew she didn't mean the money. I don't think Carol believed I would not be going out of state as often. And, she reminded me of my promise to Mama. Two days later, December 27, 1960, I was sworn in as a member of the New York City Police Department. This was another giant step in my life that I wasn't sure I was prepared for.

CHAPTER FOUR

So, at age twenty-five, I entered the New York City Police Academy. This was the beginning of a six month program of vigorous physical and academic training. I had no idea how much criminal law a police officer must retain in order to perform his duties. At the same time, we had to keep our bodies in top physical condition.

In addition to purchasing numerous books on criminal law, we were sent to downtown New York City where we purchased uniforms from a store called Smith & Grey. After being measured for the uniform, we received gray pants, a blue hat, a leather belt, and two revolvers. One revolver was a Smith & Wesson six-inch barrel, which was to be carried while on duty. The other revolver was a Smith & Wesson two-inch barrel Detective Special to be carried when off duty.

We would receive our regular winter and summer uniforms at a later date. I was under the impression that the uniforms and guns were supplied to the officers by the New York City Police Department. It was a shock to me when I was told to sign a loan agreement in the amount of five thousand dollars to cover the cost of these items. I thought to myself, shat the hell am I doing. I took this job to make money, and I just put myself in a financial hole. I had to support a wife, two small girls, pay rent, and still pay several other bills. When I received my first paycheck as a rookie, I stared at it in disbelief. After taxes and deductions, my take home pay was eighty-one dollars. I reached out to one of my instructors for some expert advice on whether or not I should stay on the job.

He said, "Cops deliver lectures, babies and bad news. They are required to have the wisdom of Solomon, the disposition of a lamb, and muscles of steel, and are often accused of having a heart to match. He's the one who rings the doorbell, swallows hard and announces the passing of a loved one. He then spends the rest of the day wondering why he ever took this job. He gets a medal for saving lives and chasing crooks, although sometimes his widow gets the medal. But the most rewarding moment comes when after a small kindness to an older person, he feels a warm handclasp, looks into grateful eyes and hears, 'Thank you and God Bless you, Son!'"

I guess my instructor's little speech brought my doubts to an end. I was going to be a New York City police officer, or should I say I was going to be a poor New York City police officer.

I went home and showed Carol my first paycheck. We sat down at the kitchen table with our monthly bills spread out in front of us. The figures didn't lie: rent, food, electricity, carfare, and so forth. There was no way we could stretch my paycheck to make ends meet. Mama had to be told about this financial hardship. I would have to tell her that I was going back to my previous job. This was not going to be easy thing to do since she had her heart set on my becoming a police officer.

After showing Mama everything in black and white, she just looked at me and smiled. She said, "No problem. All of you will move into Mama's house. You don't have to pay for rent or food. There are plenty of bedrooms. Just move my furniture into the garage, and you can put your furniture wherever you like." I was speechless and looked to Carol for an answer. Mama quickly interceded, "I will take care of the children while Carol works as a registered nurse in a hospital. You can both save money for two years. This will allow you to buy a house on Long Island."

Carol and I looked at each other, pondering Mama's offer. We agreed to this arrangement. Mama was ecstatic, and it took a heavy load off my mind. I could now concentrate on becoming one of New York's finest.

The academic training was very intense. At the gun range, you were taught the rules of when and where you could use deadly force, although this was no picnic either. A lot of time we spent in the gym learning judo and the use of our baton. We were also taught many other physical aspects of the job. I can't say that those six months went by fast. It was not an easy road, but it was certainly well worth it. This would probably be the best physical and mental condition I would ever be in.

Soon after graduating from the Police Academy, I was assigned to the Twenty-Sixth Precinct located in Harlem. Before this assignment, I had never been to Harlem. Now, this was where I was going to start my career as a street cop.

The Two-Six, as it was called, was made up of fifty percent black officers and fifty percent white officers. The desk sergeant assigned me to a foot post on Convent Avenue and 135th Street outside City College of New York. As a new officer, I was told this was a good place to start. Compared to much of New York, the streets there were quieter than many other neighborhoods. I guess the sergeant figured it was a good place for a beginner to gain some experience. I exited the station house on my way to my foot post. A few blocks away, I came upon four or five small boys who were about seven or eight years of age. They danced around me singing, "Look at the rookie. Here comes the rookie."

I thought to myself, how do these kids know I'm a rookie? I stopped and asked, "What makes you say that?"

One little guy stepped forward and said, "Your hat is new and your nightstick is shiny." I laughed and thought to myself, if I only had the street smarts these little guys have. I continued on to my post, stopping frequently to rub my nightstick on a cement or iron fence. The stick would soon look like an old one.

It was ten thirty at night when I observed three men exit a brand new Mercedes sedan. They didn't lock the car and were walking swiftly away from the automobile, so I stopped them and asked for the registration of the car and license of the driver, who stood around six-foot-two. His reply to me was "What are you jiving us for mother fucker?"

He came towards me with his hands at his side, palms open and his shoulders moving up and down. I stood there thinking, what the hell do I do now? His movements seemed threatening, especially when the other two guys also started walking towards me. I pulled my gun from my holster, and ordered all of them against the fence, which surrounded City College.

The taller one kept coming at me though, and by the looks of him, I knew that he and his friends would easily overpower me and take my gun. Then, my life would be in their hands. For a split second I had a flashback to Korea, and then I immediately turned my focus to the situation at hand. It was going to be my life or his. I looked him straight in the eyes, pointed my gun at his chest, and cocked the hammer. I was seconds away from pulling the trigger, and I had every intention of shooting this oncoming threat. I knew if he heard the double click of the hammer, he would stop. I pulled the hammer back and he did stop. His hands immediately went up in the air, as did his accomplices.

"Against the fucking fence!" I shouted.

"Okay man, we're cool!" they said as they cooperated without hesitation. Much to my relief I had the situation in hand.

I realized that my encounters on the streets would be with a different kind of enemy than I had in Korea. Their eyes are round instead of slanted; they didn't wear uniforms; and I could not see their weapons. Most important, they would kill you in order to stay out of jail. This was only one of the many lessons I would learn as a police officer.

At this time, police department two-way radios did not exist for the cop walking a beat. As luck would have it, there was a call box on the corner of 135th Street, which was not more than fifty feet away. I searched all three suspects. I had two of the suspects put one hand through the fence and then I handcuffed them together. With only one set of cuffs, I forced the other suspect, who was the shortest of the three, to kneel down by the call box with his hands clasped behind his head.

The call box and a public telephone were the only communication that a patrolman had with the station house at that time, so I made the call. The sergeant answered, and I told him that I had three suspects who needed transporting to the station house. With a surprise in his voice he asked, "How did you manage to get three suspects?" As I was about to answer he said, "Forget it." I heard him call a radio car "we have a rookie holding three possible prisoners on the corner of 135th and Convent!"

Only a few minutes had passed when I heard the siren coming in my direction. A radio car pulled up to my location and two seasoned cops exited the police car asking, "What have you got kid?" I explained what had taken place and one of them said, "Okay, but why did you think the car was stolen?" I told them that the suspects didn't lock the car after they parked it. Both cops laughed and said, "Only a rookie would come up with that one!"

They checked the license plate number with Central Dispatch. The alarm blared over the radio, "That car was stolen two days ago." A big smile appeared on my face.

The two cops said, "We'll take it from here kid. You don't want this collar. It will take a lot of paperwork."

I stood there and said, "Okay, I'm new in this command. If this way works better for all concerned, it's fine with me." They put the prisoners in the patrol car and proceeded to the station house. Later that evening when I returned to the station house, the sergeant asked me what happened to my prisoners. I told him that the patrolmen in the radio car said they would take the arrest because it required a lot of paperwork.

He looked at me, laughed and said, "Son, those two nice policemen stole a good arrest from you." I told him that it didn't matter. Another lesson learned the hard way. I would keep it in the back of my mind and not let it happen again. My tour was finished so I changed into my civilian clothes. My first day on the streets of Harlem had come to a close. It had been a long day, and I was looking forward to going home.

About one month later, I was transferred to the Nineteenth Precinct because they were short on manpower. The station house was located on East Sixty-Seventh Street between Third and Lexington Avenues. Unaware at the time, the Nineteenth Precinct was to become my home for the next fourteen years.

Here is where I would develop lifelong friendships with many of the officers of the precinct.

CHAPTER FIVE

I arrived at the Nineteenth Precinct on June 6, 1961, and met the captain along with a few sergeants. I was assigned to a squad and given a locker. Here I changed into my uniform and then proceeded to the main floor. This is where I would stand roll call and receive my assignment each day. On entering the room, I encountered two officers who introduced themselves as Joe Spinelli and Don Hart. Unaware of it at the time, these were the two men who would mold me into the police officer that I was to become in the years ahead. This was only the beginning of a friendship that would last for more than four decades.

Joe "The Spinner," as he was affectionately called, rode in a radio car with another officer covering sector George, which was from 72nd Street to 79th Street and from the East River to Fifth Avenue. Don Hart and I were assigned to an adjoining foot post on Lexington Avenue. I would do foot patrol from 67th Street to 77th Street. Don Hart's post was from 77th Street to 86th Street. There were numerous times when we would meet on 77th Street. We would go into Lenox Hill Hospital Emergency Room for a cup of coffee and have a chat with the doctors and nurses.

When we were not assigned to a foot post, we would pull the terribly dreaded boring duty of guarding a foreign embassy. The Nineteenth Precinct had the so-called honor of guarding the Russian Embassy. This was always a problem because of our unstable relationship with the Russian government. My precinct covered about twenty foreign embassies, with the Cuban and

Russian as the most important. When we pulled this detail, we stood in front of the embassy like a cigar store wooden Indian. It was an eight hour shift. We stood seven hours in front of the building and had one hour for a meal. The summer wasn't bad, but winter brought the cold wind coming out of Central Park. This made for a long shift. Once in a while, the sector car would come by with a container of coffee. Believe me, it was well appreciated.

Don Hart and I hit it off right away since we had a lot in common. He was a year older than me, but we were both born in January. He also had two children. He had been in the Marine Corps and served in Korea. We never spoke too much about our times in Korea. It was a part of our lives we had chosen to put behind us.

We were teamed together as partners, and after a few months of working together, we were known by our fellow officers as "the two D.H.s." There were three different working shifts in the precinct: one week of midnight to eight in the morning; one week of eight in the morning to four in the afternoon; and one week of four in the afternoon to midnight. The last was the best shift according to all the officers in the precinct. When this shift was over, we would head down to Kenny Byers Cocktail Lounge located on 71st Street between First and York Avenues. There we could escape the stress of the job, just sit around and have a couple of cold beers. Usually on our last shift, the stopover at Kenny Byers turned out to be what was commonly known as "the four to four shift."

Kenny Byers was the place where cops told each other stories about what took place during the week. I later learned that this was done so we wouldn't take the pressures of the job home with us and put undo stress on our families. I enjoyed this ritual. It was right up my alley.

It was a hot day in June, and I was working the four to twelve shift. I was assigned to First Avenue around 67th Street. A woman approached me and told me that there were men fighting on 69th Street and First Avenue. When I arrived there were three young men all in their twenties, fist fighting on the sidewalk. As I intervened, one fellow hit me in the chest sending me backwards into a storefront plate glass window. My only fear was that the thick plate glass window would break as I went through it, and for a moment I imagined the broken glass slicing me in half. Thank God, the glass didn't break. I bounced off of it swinging my nightstick like a musician conducting an orchestra. I caught one of the brawlers in the knee with my nightstick and he went down. Seeing this, the other two men stopped fighting immediately. A radio car pulled up and Officer George Cavanaugh exited the car. George was a big man who took shit from no one. I placed the three men under arrest, and we transported them to the station house.

At the station house I learned that two of the fighters were brothers, Kevin and Frank, and the other man was a cousin. They were moving furniture from their apartment and drinking beer when an argument broke out between all three. I told the desk lieutenant that I was only interested in locking up Kevin, the one who had struck me. The lieutenant asked if the arrest was for assaulting an officer, which is a felony, or disorderly conduct, which is a misdemeanor. I answered, "Disorderly conduct."

He then told Frank and his cousin to go home. When they left the station house, the lieutenant took me to the side and said, "Son, you just made a mistake. The two that you cut loose will be witnesses against you in court."

Later, we made night court with time to spare. I put Kevin in the holding pen to wait for our docket number to be called. As we waited Kevin told me that he was married, and expecting his first child in a few months. I told him that he would probably get fined and go home in a few hours. Our number was called, and we stood before the judge. He imposed a five-dollar fine or five days in jail. Kevin replied, "I don't even have a dollar on me."

The judge replied, "Put him in jail, Officer."

I escorted Kevin back to the holding cell and noticed that he was crying. I stopped and put a five-dollar bill in his hand. I said to him, "Tell them you just found it in your back pocket." Again we went before the judge where Kevin produced the five-dollar bill. The judge looked at me, but I would not let our eyes meet.

The judge said, "You're free to go!"

I drove Kevin home. He shook my hand and thanked me. Years later, I met his brother, Frank. To my surprise, he had become a police officer. He thanked me for not arresting him on that hot day in June. If I had he would not have qualified to be a police officer. I recalled the lieutenant telling me on that day that I had made a big mistake by not arresting all three of them. I thought to myself, "I guess I didn't make a big mistake." I found it weird how things work out in the crazy world we live in.

It was last evening shift for D. H. and me for a while. When it was over, I would be going on a two-week vacation. I was looking forward to this time off because Carol was due to have our third child. D.H. and I were stopped for a red light on 79th Street and Second Avenue when an elderly woman came to the car window. She informed us that the young man in the car ahead of us had just spit a large spitball on her. I got out of the car and approached the driver in his car. I asked him to exit the vehicle. After explaining to him what I knew, I asked him to apologize to the woman. He said, "That's tough shit. She was in the wrong place when I spit out the window."

I asked for his license and registration, which he reluctantly gave to me. I examined the vehicle and informed him that he was being issued a summons for not having a license plate light. He laughed out loud and said, "Who cares?" I wrote the summons and handed it to him. As he took it from my hand, he turned to a crowd of people who had gathered around the scene and said, "Watch this."

He ripped the summons into very small pieces and flung it into the air. I starred at him, opened my summons book and wrote him a summons for littering. He crumbled it up and threw it onto the roadway. I calmly put the summons book in my back pocket and took out the handcuffs. I said, "Okay wise guy. You're now under arrest for disorderly conduct."

As I placed him in the radio car, the crowd began clapping and cheering in support of my actions. We took him to the station house, made out the proper paperwork, and went to night court. The young man was not as brave once he lost his audience. He was very quiet and scared. The judge, who was not pleased with his actions, read him the riot act. He was fined two hundred and fifty dollars for littering and twenty-five dollars for disorderly conduct. He was given a date to appear in court for the vehicle violation.

It was time to go back to the station house to sign out and start my vacation. Before I left I said to D.H., "I can't believe that I'm being paid for something that I love to do." D.H. laughed and said to call him when the baby was born. I nodded a yes and headed home to Mama's house.

CHAPTER SIX

On June 24, 1961, my third daughter, Colleen, was born. We were now a family of five living in Mama's house. Things were going just the way Mama and I had planned them. Two years had passed and Carol was working as an emergency room nurse. And I had finally received my final increment of top pay in the department. We did exactly what Mama had said to do and we had saved a little money. Carol and I didn't go out much or go on expensive vacations, but we always managed to slip Mama some money. Of course, it wasn't nearly enough to compensate her for the all the things she had done for us.

Then one day I received a phone call from Dick Butler. He had been in Korea with me, and now he was down from Troy, New York, for a couple of days with his wife to see the big city. He was hoping I didn't have any plans because he wanted to see me. I gave him directions, and about an hour later he and his beautiful wife arrived for a visit. We were sitting in the living room with a couple of beers talking about old times. Butler told me that he was a New York State Trooper, and he couldn't believe that I had become a New York City Police Officer. We both found it odd that although we had not seen each other since Korea, the two of us chose law enforcement.

A short time had passed when Butler handed me a bankbook along with a check for the amount of eight thousand dollars. The bankbook revealed that there was a balance of sixteen thousand dollars. I looked at Butler and said, "I don't understand, what is this?"

Butler had tears in his eyes and replied, "I wouldn't be sitting here if it wasn't for you. I told you that day in Korea, everything I made for the rest of my life would be half yours."

I got up from the chair that I was sitting in and started crying. I started ripping the check into little pieces. I said, "Right and if you remember, I told you that same day you have things a little backwards, you saved me!"

We hugged and cried together, standing over those little pieces of paper. After dinner, Butler and his wife wanted to get back to the big city and continue their vacation. We said our goodbyes, and off they went. When they left I thought to myself, what an incredible life I am living.

My sister, Alice, and her husband, Tom, had bought a house on Long Island. Carol, the kids, and I drove out to see the place. It was in the town of Farmingdale. They called this style of house a ranch because it is all on one level. I had heard the Farmingdale School District was an excellent one. When we arrived at their house, it was still in the process of being built. As I looked around the property, I noticed directly across the street was a sprawling ranch house that had a "For Sale By Owner Sign" on the lawn. The house was three bedrooms, one bath, with a one car garage and was located on a half acre of land.

I asked the price, and the owner told me nineteen thousand five hundred. I offered nineteen thousand two fifty and was told that he wouldn't sell the house for less than nineteen thousand three hundred. I agreed to his price, and wrote a check for the deposit.

We drove home and told Mama the good news. She was happy and sad at the same time. Sad that we would be moving out, and that the kids to whom she had become very attached would be so far away. I told Mama that if it wasn't for her offer to take us in for two years, we never could have afforded to buy anything, let alone a house. Mama smiled and kissed us both.

It was far for me to drive to visit with Mama and also to drive to work since the house was twenty-six miles from Mama's house and thirty-five miles to the precinct. I was a bit nervous knowing I would now have a house and all the responsibilities that go with it—a mortgage, utility bills, and all the other bills that come with a family life. Everything worked out though, and we moved into our first house the very next month. The kids loved it because they had my sister, Alice, and her two kids across the street. My knowledge of carpentry came in handy when we decided to expand the house.

A short time later, I expanded the sixty-five foot ranch to eighty-five feet in length. I made it into a four bedroom ranch with a two and a half car garage. I constructed a big patio in the back yard and put in a very large above ground pool for the kids. The house was beautiful, and I was on cloud nine.

My brother, Billy, also lived in Farmingdale a few miles away, and it was Billy who found the house for Alice. My father no longer drove a car due to his bad health. So sometimes, I picked up Mama and Dad on the way home from work and they would stay at our house for the weekend. My brother with his three kids, Alice and her kids, and some of my cousins and their kids would all show up for another weekend barbeque at the Harleys. All had a good time, and my house became known as "Harleys Ponderosa."

Months had passed and winter brought the snow. New York City looked beautiful covered in white, and the snow was still coming down pretty heavy that Sunday morning. Don Hart and I were assigned to a radio car. The radio was very quiet, and there were not many reports coming over the air due to the inclement weather. Since it was so slow, we decided to pull a prank on the other sector car. Pranks of this nature were our specialty. Of course, you had to be sure the recipients of the prank were good sports. Mike Hughes and Eddie Rack were partners in the other sector car. Mike was a tall Irishman, and we knew these guys could take a joke. This was important because believe me, you do not want Mike Hughes mad at you.

We called Central and said that we would like to talk to a police officer about some property that we had lost. We gave the address to an apartment building on Fifth Avenue, which was located on the fourteenth floor. In the meantime, D.H. and I parked our car about a block away so we could watch when Mike and Eddie arrived with their radio car. Within minutes we saw their car park directly in front of the building. They got out of the car and spoke to the doorman, who was shoveling snow from the walkway, before moving to the door. They entered the building and were on their way up to the non-existent job on the fourteenth floor. We quickly drove up to the building, parking directly behind their radio car. The doorman was an elderly gentleman dressed in his uniform, overcoat, and hat. He was shoveling away the deep snow for his tenants to have a clear path to the sidewalk.

We approached him and asked, "Where are the two officers that were in that car?"

The doorman said, "They just went upstairs, do you want me to get them?"

I turned to D.H. and said, "We'll never make it now. We have to be at Park Avenue in seven minutes." The doorman was leaning on the handle of the shovel with a look of bewilderment on his face. I said to him, "Maybe you could help us?"

He answered, "Sure thing, Officer."

I then explained to him that Mayor Lindsay wanted two samples of snow, one from Fifth Avenue and one from Park Avenue. I said to him, "My partner and I will put the snow in the car. When the officers come down would you tell them to drive the snow down to Mayor Lindsay's office right away. That would really save us a lot of time."

The doorman said, "I'll be glad to!"

I then asked him if I could borrow his shovel. He was very accommodating. We opened the driver's door and the rear door and began filling the car with snow. We filled it from the top of the rear seat to the top of the front seat and closed the door. Then we filled the passenger seat from the top of the seat to the dashboard, leaving the driver's seat free of any snow.

I handed the shovel back to the doorman, thanked him and said, "We have to get over to Park Avenue now for another sample. Be sure to tell the officers to deliver this right away."

He waved his hand in the air and yelled, "Will do."

We drove away and sped around the block. We parked in our original spot, which was a block away. This allowed us to observe Mike and Eddie as they came out of the building. Even before they got to their car, I had a pain in my side from laughing.

A short time passed and Mike and Eddie emerged from the apartment building. They walked past the doorman who did not see them come out of the building, and they immediately spotted the snow in the radio car. Mike and Eddie turned towards the doorman, who was leaning on the tall handle of the shovel bidding his time until called on to give the two officers their orders. The doorman saw the expressions on their faces. It finally dawned on him, these officers think that I put the snow in their car.

He immediately dropped the shovel to the ground. We observed him from our car, frantically motioning with his arms and hands to explain how this incident had developed. He then pointed downtown, continuing with his explanations. We knew this was to inform the officers where we were headed at the end of this scenario. The doorman threw his arms in the air as if to say, what the hell did I get myself into here? I don't understand!

D.H. and I slowly cruised by Mike and Eddie, as they were attempting to remove the snow from the car. We were doubled over with pain from laughing. We waved and continued down the avenue. I said to D.H., "They have to get every bit of snow out of the car before they turn their heater on, or they will be in a swimming pool."

This thought only brought on more laughter. We knew we would have to be on our guard from here on in, because they were sure to retaliate. After stopping at a deli, we picked up lunch and headed down to the 59th Street Sanitation Pier on the East River, where we joined Joe Spinner. The three of us had lunch. We told Joe about the prank on Mike and Eddie. He laughed so hard that he spilled coffee all over his pants. The laughter was endless. What a day!

Our lunch was interrupted by Central with a "possible DOA at 445 East 65th Street in apartment twelve." Our lunch went into the nearest garbage pail. We proceeded to the address, which we knew was a walk-up old tenement. We could smell death as soon as we walked into the building. It always amazed me that neighbors would wait so long to call the police, when the smell of a decaying body was so obvious. The tenants met us and pointed out apartment twelve. They told us that the man lived alone, and had no living relatives. I thought to myself, what a way to go. No one to grieve over his departing this world. The city would bury him in Potter's Field, along with all the other poor souls who had no families to bury them.

Don Hart put his shoulder to the door forcing the lock to break open. The putrid stench hit us in the face like a sledge hammer. I covered my nose and mouth with a handkerchief. I asked a neighbor if she would mind burning some coffee grinds in an old pot and bringing it in to us. I explained to her that this would alleviate some of the odor. When we found him, the old man was lying on the kitchen floor covered with flesh-eating maggots. Parts of his face and body had already been eaten away. It was terrible thinking about what happens to someone when no one cares. The poor guy had to have been dead for at least three weeks.

We called for a sergeant. He arrived at the scene with attendants from the morgue and a medical examiner. Naturally, they pronounced the body dead. It seems like such a waste of time when it's obvious the guy isn't getting up again, but you have to follow procedure. Everyone left the apartment in a hurry as soon as they could leave. D.H. and I stayed while the morgue attendants placed the body in a black body bag. There was an old toaster on the kitchen counter. One of the attendants turned to me and said, "Hey, Officer, can I have that toaster? Mine broke yesterday, and my wife and I really need one. With the pay we get, I can't just run out and get a new one."

I looked at him and said, "You've got to be shitting me. I can't let you walk out of here with a toaster under your arm."

He said, "No look, I'll just put it in here." With that he placed the toaster in the body bag along the side of the dead body, which was still covered with maggots, and zippered up the bag, squashing a few maggots in the zipper during this process.

I looked at D.H. and said, "Let's get the hell out of here!" We secured the apartment, and we informed the neighbors that the owner of the building would have to get rid of the meager belongings that were left in the apartment.

When we got in the car, I said to D. H., "I'll bet that creepy attendant is going to cook his wife bacon and eggs in the morning with a little toast on the side."

After being exposed to the smell of a ripe DOA, it was common for us to drive to the nearest bar. When you handled a ripe one, the smell stayed in your nostrils and mouth. The only way to get rid of it was to eat bitters and lemon. We pulled up to O'Brian's Café. The bartender, whom we called "Light Lunch," since he was very large and overweight, greeted us as we asked for two bitters and lemon. He looked at us and said, "Guess you guys had another bad one." After eating it, we washed it down with a few drinks and headed back to the station house to sign off duty and call it a day.

CHAPTER SEVEN

It was some years later, and Joe Spinelli was asked to head the community relations department in the precinct. He would be in civilian clothes, speaking to large groups from the community. Joe had made arrangements with the desk lieutenant for Don Hart and me to drive him downtown to Macy's department store. There he was going to speak on community relations. It was a very cold day, about ten thirty in the morning, when D.H. and I had stopped for a red light located on Broadway and 45th Street. Don Hart was driving, and I was in the passenger seat, commonly known as the recorder seat. A gentleman approached the car and knocked on my window. I rolled down the window, and he excitedly blurted out, "A man just robbed my jewelry store, and there he is!" I stepped out of the car and saw the subject start to run from the store.

I started to run after him. He turned the corner and headed west on 45th Street. I was about a half a block behind him when I saw him turn towards me and pause with his right arm extended and pointed directly at me. I thought to myself, thank God! He's giving up. I was out of breath from running. It was then that I heard the sound from his gun. He had stopped long enough to aim and fire at me. From experience, I knew that when you hear the report from a gun, the bullet has already passed you. I wasn't taking any chances. I jumped into a doorway entrance fearful he would try to take another shot at me, since this one might find it's mark. I looked out from the doorway entrance and I saw that he was on the run again. He had now put a considerable amount of distance between us.

A taxicab was just passing by me. I put my hand up to stop him. I jumped into the passenger seat and told the driver to pull up the street to the far corner. He observed the gun in my hand and said, "No! I don't want any trouble!"

I said, "You'll know what trouble is if you don't do what I tell you."

With that in mind, he pushed his foot on the gas pedal. We were at the corner in a flash. The cab driver quickly lay down on the front seat, as I jumped out of his cab. The subject was on the sidewalk, opposite me. He was looking up the street, trying to figure out where I had disappeared to so fast. I leaned over the hood of the taxicab and sighted my revolver on his chest. Now I had a decision to make. Do I shoot him right away because he tried to kill me, or do I yell police? It felt like a voice on my right was saying, "Shoot him," and the voice on my left was saying, "Give him a warning, then shoot him."

It was déjà vu, happening again, just as it did in Korea when I was faced with shooting someone. And just like in Korea, everything was flashing before me in slow motion. Snapping out of it, I yelled, "Freeze, and drop your gun!"

He looked at me, turned and ran off again at full speed. I cursed myself for hesitating. I took off after him. I heard a fellow police officer behind me, who had joined the pursuit, shout, "Let one go at him!"

Although the officer wanted me to fire a shot, I felt that there was too much distance between us. I wasn't confident that I could hit him while we were on the run. If I missed, which I was sure would happen, my bullet would continue straight ahead and hit an innocent bystander.

We had run about two city blocks when I contemplated firing a warning shot in the air. I wanted the subject to know that I wasn't going to let him get away. I could see the Hudson River about two blocks ahead. I knew that if I fired in the air, my bullet would follow an angle about a half-mile and then drop into the Hudson River. This, of course, was against all department rules of engagement. We were never allowed to fire a warning shot. Still, I decided this would be better than killing an innocent bystander.

As I was still running, I pointed my revolver in the air and fired a warning shot. What a fucking disaster! As it turned out, when I fired my gun, I was running under a theatre marquee. The bullet shattered the marquee above me, and glass rained down on my head. Pedestrians took cover at the sound of the gunfire. The situation looked like a movie from the Keystone Kops. I recovered my composure and continued the chase. I spotted the perpetrator running in the street on the next block. He was attempting to go between two parked cars when he tripped and fell. His gun slid under the parked car, and he was trying to retrieve it, lying face down, reaching for the gun, when I came up behind him. I put my gun to the back of his head and said, "If you move another muscle, I'll blow your fucking head off!"

My lungs were bursting in my chest, but I managed to handcuff the bastard just as D.H. arrived on the scene. Don Hart put the subject in the radio car, and we proceeded back to the jewelry store to pick up the storeowner, who would accompany us to the Eighteenth Precinct. Meanwhile, Joe took public transportation to reach his destination.

I charged the defendant with attempted murder of a police officer, robbery, resisting arrest, and possession of a firearm. It was later that I was informed that the gun the subject used had been taken from an off-duty police officer. The police officer still had a broken jaw, after being mugged on Christmas Eve. While D.H. and I were making out the paperwork, a duty captain was called to the station house. This was normal procedure when shots had been fired. I was sent to see the captain in his office.

He asked me if I was aware of the rule, which required police officers to never fire a warning shot. I admitted that I was aware of the rule and tried to explain to the captain the extenuating circumstances of this particular incident. The captain shook his head, of course. He said, "You should receive a complaint and be fined two days pay. However, since you retrieved a police officer's revolver, I am just going to enter in your service record that you were warned and admonished."

He looked at me, waiting for a thank you, but that wasn't going to happen. I felt like I was the criminal. D.H. and I returned to our command with utter disgust of the system. At a later date, the defendant went before a judge and received a five-year sentence for his crime, big fucking deal!

Although Don Hart and I did not agree with some of the rules and regulations of the department, or the lenient sentences given to some of the criminals, we were still proud to be New York City police officers. During the summer months, D.H. and I spent most of our days off at the beach in Breezy Point, Brooklyn, with our wives and kids. Don Hart moonlighted as a lifeguard at the Fort Tilden Army Base, which was located at Breezy Point Beach. He had the police department's approval to moonlight, as was required by policy. Carol and I, along with our three girls, and Joan and her two boys, Kenny and Rickie, would meet at the beach. I had no trouble getting on the army base because D.H. would leave passes with the soldier on duty at the main gate.

There were times when we only saw D.H. from a distance. He would be far out in the water doing his workout. He would swim back and forth for hours. He was an extremely strong swimmer and enjoyed the ocean. This was "his thing" so we were never insulted when he didn't come ashore. The kids enjoyed Breezy Point, as we all did. When D.H. would finally come out of the water, we would pack up and head for Kennedy's Restaurant for a few drinks and a delicious dinner.

On my days off that weren't spent at Breezy Point, I worked on finishing my basement. It was always my dream to have a basement with a large beautiful bar where I could entertain the guys from the precinct. I always wanted to throw parties that they would never forget. A few more days of hard work, and the basement would be completed.

CHAPTER EIGHT

I went back to work on the four to twelve shift and was riding with D.H. We had pulled up to 67th Street and Second Avenue, when I spotted Harvey standing on the corner with his thumb in his mouth. Harvey was about twenty-two years old. He lived with his mother and his sister, who was a few years older than him. They lived in a fourth floor walk-up on Second Avenue. Most officers from the precinct, at one time or another, had handled disputes in this apartment building. Both Harvey and his sister were more than slightly retarded. They were a handful for their eight-five year old mother.

I pulled the radio car along side of Harvey. I leaned out the window and said, "How are you doing, Harvey? I hope your not peeing in the coffee pot anymore?" His mother had a large camp-style coffee pot, which she would leave on the stove. Whenever Harvey got the urge to urinate, he would pee in the coffee pot. Due to her age and ill health, Harvey's mother was bedridden for most of the day. He and his sister would try to take care of her. D.H. and I had reported this situation on numerous occasions, to the Welfare Department. To this date, however, nothing had been investigated.

I said to Harvey, "Where is your sister, and why aren't you upstairs?"

Harvey looked at me and said, "My sister went to the store for milk. She's mad at me because I did peepee in the coffee pot. My

47

mother yelled at me too, but I showed her. I lit a candle and put it under her bed."

I said, "You did what!" I immediately looked up at the fourth floor. I yelled to D.H. "Holy Shit!" The flames were shooting out of the window like an inferno. I picked up the radio and called Central. I informed them that we had an apartment ablaze and gave them the location.

I asked Harvey, "Where's your mother?"

He replied, "In bed, where do you think she is?"

D.H. and I raced up the four flights and opened the apartment door. You couldn't see your hand in front of you. The black smoke from the burning mattress engulfed the entire apartment. I knew the location of the mother's bedroom from my previous visits.

She was screaming, "Help me! Please help me! I'm burning! Please, please help me!"

I ran towards the screams. I made it to her doorway, and then I couldn't go any further. I had inhaled too much smoke and was unable to breathe. I turned back to the kitchen. As a black mucous dripped from my nose and soot coughed up from my lungs, I motioned to D.H. to go for her. Don Hart got down on his hands and knees and crawled into the smoke-filled hallway. But he also returned coughing and spitting, and without the old lady. We looked at each other and I said, "We can't let her die like this. We'll both go. Maybe, one of us will be able to grab her."

We both ran down the hallway. We didn't even get as far as we did the first time. We once again returned on our knees. Our faces were covered with mucous and soot, and we were coughing up a storm. We were not able to reach her. We looked up, and there stood a New York City fireman in the kitchen. I pointed down the hallway, and told him that he would need a scott pack with oxygen to get to the woman. He calmly walked past me and strolled down the hallway, returning with the frail old woman in his arms. He laid her on a stretcher.

He turned to me and D.H. and me and said, "Either of you guys have a cigarette?"

I looked at him in amazement, as I handed him a Lucky Strike cigarette. I said to him, "Thank God you got here when you did. There was no way we would have been able to get to her."

The fireman laughed and said, "Have a good day, Officers." He then walked down the stairs of the tenement.

We followed feeling very proud of the man walking in front of us. We didn't need any bitters and lemon this time, but we sure did need a nice cold drink. Joe Gleason's Saloon was our destination. We met Joe, the owner, and told him the story of the fireman. While we were there we noticed it was our meal period, so we settled in for a bite to eat.

We were sitting in a booth finishing our meal when Patty Quinn walked in the front door. Patty was one of the bartenders that worked at Gleason's Restaurant. Patty's antics behind the bar were ones that had to be seen to be appreciated. It was Patty's day off. He was dressed in a tuxedo with white spats and white gloves. He went directly to the bar and bought a round of drinks for everyone standing at the bar. He knew most of them since they were his regulars. When it came to spending money, Patty was no slouch. He spotted D.H. and me and came over to shake our hands. I asked him, "Why the hell are you all decked out?" He said he was dressed for bar hopping in the stretch limo but his chauffeur didn't appreciate all the stops.

All of a sudden Patty clapped his hands together and said, "I've got a great idea! You guys leave and park up the block on York Avenue. When we pass you, pull the limo over for a violation. I'll then talk you out of giving the driver a summons. He will love me for the rest of the night."

Patty knew that we were known to do anything for a laugh. Naturally, we agreed. We left Gleason's through the side door. Our car was parked on the side street, out of the driver's view. We waited in the car and watched as Patty left the restaurant. The limo started north on York Avenue. We followed for about a block. We then put the turret lights on and gave a short blast with the siren. The driver immediately pulled over to the curb. D.H. and I approached the driver's window and asked him to exit the car, along with his passenger in the rear seat. We placed them against an iron fence. We told the driver that his passenger had just picked up two kilos of heroin from the restaurant they had just left.

I explained, "You are now an accomplice to this act."

The driver frantically exclaimed, "I'm only a driver! I don't even know this guy!"

I replied, "It doesn't matter because the drugs are in your limo."

They both had their backs to us, arms in the air and were holding onto the fence. Patty was looking at us as if to say, it was only supposed to be a traffic stop. Just then, another radio car that was passing, stopped and put their turret lights on. The two cops approached us. We knew one of them. He was nicknamed "Crash" because of his many accidents. He asked, "What do you have here?"

I looked at him and said, "We have them." I leaned over to Don Hart and whispered, "Let's leave." We got in our car and left Crash with his hands on his hips and the so-called prisoners.

Patty, not noticing that we had left, looked over his shoulders, and then he turned to the panic-stricken driver and said, "Oh shit! These guys aren't the fun cops." The driver had no idea what Patty was talking about.

About thirty minutes later, D.H. and I saw Patty's limo double-parked in front of Mr. Laff's restaurant. We went inside and saw Patty and his driver at the bar. When Patty saw us, he broke out into a fit of laughter. "You fucking guys! It took me twenty minutes to explain to the cop that I was a friend of the two D.H.s, and this was a practical joke."

Meanwhile, the driver was down at the end of the bar having a drink to calm himself down. I said to Patty, "If your driver keeps that up, you will be driving and the chauffeur will be sitting in the rear seat." After a few more laughs, D.H. and I headed back to patrol.

Central told us to respond to the lower level of the Queensborough Bridge, where there was a four-car accident. We arrived at the scene and found the traffic was backed up on the bridge. I notified central and asked them to have Queens precinct close off the lower level of the bridge. There was only one lane open to vehicles passing the accident. It became evident that an eastbound vehicle had crossed over the divider, and collided head-on with a westbound taxicab. Don Hart began to collect the licenses from the driver's of the three vehicles. I went over to the taxicab.

There was a man sitting in the back sit, who appeared to be in shock. His eyes were wide open, and he was staring straight ahead. I opened the rear door and asked him if he was hurt. He didn't reply, so I placed my hand on his shoulder and said, "Mister, are you all right?"

When I touched him, he fell over onto his side. I checked for a pulse. There was none. The man was dead. I pulled him back into a sitting position. I worked my way back to D.H. and asked, "Where the hell is the cab driver?"

D.H. looked at all the credentials in his possession and said, "I don't have the cab driver's license."

I told D.H., "We've got to find him because there is a dead guy in the back seat of the cab." When I went back to the cab, I noticed that the dead guy was not wearing any shoes or socks. I opened the driver's door and saw a pair of sandals. One sandal was by the gas pedal and the other was alongside the brake pedal. I looked at the picture on the hack license. I was in complete awe. The man in the back seat was the cab driver. The cab did not have a partition separating the front from the back, and the force of the collision threw him into the back seat, landing him in a sitting position.

I returned to D.H. and said, "You're not going to believe this. The impact of the head-on collision was so severe that it sent the cab driver into the back seat, knocking him right out of his sandals."

D.H. looked at me and said, "You've got to be shitting me."

"Come see for yourself!" We both examined the cab, and I put a call into Central to have a sergeant, along with the Detective Squad, respond to the scene for further investigation.

The ambulance from New York Hospital arrived and attended to the injured. They returned shortly to transport the DOA to the hospital. Tow trucks began taking the vehicles off the bridge. The sanitation department was cleaning up the glass and other debris on the roadway. Traffic was beginning to flow freely again. After wrapping this up, we drove to the hospital to get the information and diagnosis of the injured.

As we left the hospital, en route to the station house, I said to D.H., "This accident was one for Ripley's "Believe It or Not!" Don Hart nodded in agreement.

Now we faced the terrible task of calling the cab driver's family to inform them of his death. This was a part of our job that we never looked forward to doing. By the time we completed all the paperwork, our shift was over and we left the station house. After a day like this one, we both looked forward to going home to our families.

CHAPTER NINE

"Sergeant Perfect" was the name we gave him. He was tall with broad shoulders. His uniform was pressed military style with the creases sewn in permanently. He went strictly by the book. If you were not doing the job his way, you were doing it the wrong way. Most important of all, he didn't like Don Hart or Don Herlihy.

When we worked with Sergeant Perfect our main mission was to stay out of his way. We assumed he didn't care for us because he thought our pranks were very unprofessional. He made it very clear to us that if he caught us off base, he would give us both a complaint. This would result in a loss of pay. He knew we were good cops, but definitely not his class of cop.

We avoided him like the bubonic plague. Inevitably, one day we made a dreadful mistake. We stopped in O'Brian's Café to say hello. We were only there about five minutes, when I saw through the front window, the sergeant's car stopped and looked into the café. It was obvious that he spotted our car parked on the side street.

Pointing to the front window and the sergeant, I nudged D.H. and said, "We've got trouble."

Minutes later, a call from Central came over on the radio ordering us to "respond to the station house and meet with your sergeant."

I said to D.H., "What excuse are we going to give him for being in the bar?"

Don Hart smiled and said, "We'll think of something."

On our way to the station house a cab driver flagged us down. He was holding a .45 caliber handgun by the barrel. He told us that a short time ago he had dropped off a passenger. He had just noticed the gun on the back seat. I took the gun and examined it. I removed the full clip of bullets. And then I asked the cab driver to park his vehicle and accompany us to the station house. I promised him that it would not take long, and we would bring him right back to his cab.

We pulled up to the station house. There, waiting for us, stood Sergeant Perfect on the steps hands on his hip and a stern look on his face. I stepped out of the rear seat of the car with the cab driver. I placed my hand on his elbow and gently escorted him into the house. As I walked up the steps, I looked at Sergeant Perfect and said, "I've got a cab driver with a .45 caliber gun and I have to see the desk lieutenant."

I continued to walk up the steps, passing the sergeant. He stood there with a bewildered look on his face. I purposely left out the fact that all I really had was what we called "found property." I heard the sergeant say to another cop, "I had these two guys by their balls, and somehow they come up with a gun collar. They're fucking unbelievable!"

Then he went back on patrol. D.H. and I smiled at each other. We both knew that was a close call. We completed the paperwork and drove the cab driver back to his cab. We knew now that the sergeant would be relentless in his pursuit to catch us off base.

Mary Manning Walsh was a home for the elderly. Many influential people were living there. It was located on 71st Street and York Avenue. It was run by Catholic nuns. Upon its completion, Don Hart and I stopped in during our day tour to see how the finished project turned out. We were met by Mother Superior who took pride in showing us around the home. She told us she was especially proud of their cocktail lounge. Almost simultaneously, D.H. and I said, "You have a cocktail lounge?" Mother Superior took us to a sub-basement where she showed us the most beautiful cocktail lounge you ever saw. There were residents sitting in wheel chairs and walkers alongside tables as we walked to the bar. Mother Superior introduced us to the bartender, whose name was Marty. She excused herself as she had business to finish.

We were about to order a drink when Marty turned to us and said, "Officers, I hope you don't mind, but I have to charge you twenty-five cents per drink."

I put a ten-dollar bill on the bar. I turned around and announced, "We would like to buy everyone in the room a drink!"

From all parts of the room I heard, "I'll have a martini."

"Make mine a gimlet."

"A Rob Roy over here."

Marty said, "Hold on! I will get everyone their drinks. These drinks are on the officers, the two D.H.s." As Marty was serving the drinks, they all clapped their hands and raised their glasses high to show their appreciation. Don Hart and I became heroes for twenty-five cents.

What better hideaway could two cops ask for than a cocktail lounge surrounded by nuns and elderly people? We had found paradise!" Whenever we had time, we would park the car in front of Mary Manning Walsh Home and stop in to say hello to our new friends.

Sergeant Perfect had spotted our car, on many occasions, parked outside the home. Of course, he confronted us on the issue. We told him that on our meal hour, we would stop by and help the nuns get the elderly around in wheel chairs. His face lit up as if to say, "I had these two guys all wrong!" We made a friend.

What happened next was totally unexpected. While standing at roll call, Sergeant Perfect addressed the outgoing platoon. He told them how Hart and Herlihy gave up their meal hour to help the nuns, at the Mary Manning Walsh Home, a residence for elderly people. He ended his little speech, "You men should take a lesson from Hart and Herlihy."

We couldn't believe our ears. For that matter, no one on the outgoing shift could believe it either. I could hear the guys who knew us laughing and mumbling, "If the two D.H.s were being kind to a nun, they must have an ulterior motive." Of course, no one had any idea about the cocktail lounge in the sub-basement. It was now a tradition, whenever we stopped there, that we would buy a drink for all the residents in the lounge. In fact, the clientele had doubled since our first encounter.

About a year had passed. We had no further problems with Sergeant Perfect. One day he told us that he was retiring. He said, "This is my last day on the job. I've decided to ride with you guys for my last tour."

My look to D.H. was one of disbelief. It was just as I had feared when we first visited the sub-basement. Our meal hour approached and the sergeant said, "Are we going to help the nuns today?" I was silently praying that we would get a call from Central, but that was not going to happen.

Mother Superior greeted us at the door, as always, and said, "They're waiting for you men downstairs." I noticed the sergeant's chest stick out a little more than usual. Don Hart and I walked through the swinging doors with the sergeant directly behind us.

As we entered the hall, a resident yelled out, "Here come the Irish cops!" Everyone, at that point, raised their drinks in the air.

I heard the Sergeant say, as he walked behind me, "I don't believe this. You guys have been pulling the wool over my eyes for a year and a half."

I quickly responded, "Hey, Sarge, just look at all the people we made happy in their golden years." He turned around and saw some of the residents waving at him.

He said, "Yeah, you're right. What the hell. It's my last day. If anyone asks...I was never here."

With that, we all toasted him on his retirement. After we left the home, he wanted to be dropped off back at the station house. As he walked up the steps, he was shaking his head. I guess his thoughts were "the quicker I get away from these guys, the less chance I have of getting in trouble."

The shift ended and I headed for home. When I arrived, there was a letter waiting for me from the U.S. Army. They informed me that if I would like to go to college and further my education, the Veteran Administration would pay ten thousand dollars towards this education. I jumped at the opportunity. I signed up for courses in criminal justice at the New York Institute of Technology. It took me three years, but I earned an associate degree, only twenty-six credits short of a bachelor's degree. I planned to finish at a later date.

On July 30, 1965, Carol gave birth to our son, Donald. Carol, our three daughters, and I were delighted to have a little boy in the family. I now had four kids and not a hell of a lot of money. I started moonlighting as a carpenter. I insulated new homes on my days off. This would enable me to take the family on a well-deserved vacation.

Carol's aunt owned a bungalow in Point Pleasant, New Jersey. We were to go there and spend two weeks at the seashore. We worked out a deal where I did some repairs on her house while vacationing, in exchange for not paying rent.

This house was located one block from the beach, right on the Atlantic Ocean. We spent our days on the beach and our nights were spent at Seaside Heights Amusement Park. There, the kids enjoyed the rides. The kids had two weeks of fun, sand, ocean and rides. It was like they were in a world of their own. As with all vacations, it soon came to an end. It was time go back to work.

CHAPTER TEN

It was my first day back at work after the vacation. I was riding with D.H. when we received a call from Central to respond to an aided case, a possible psycho. When we arrived at the location, the mother of the aided case said that she couldn't handle her daughter's violent behavior any longer. We spoke to the girl, who was about twenty-five years of age. She was not making a bit of sense. We decided to have the ambulance take her directly to Bellevue Hospital. This was a hospital for the mentally disturbed. I informed her mother that I would have to handcuff her daughter's hands behind her back to prevent her from hurting herself. This wasn't a problem for the mother. She was just relieved that her daughter would be getting the medical attention that she so desperately needed.

The ambulance attendant strapped the daughter on a gurney lying on her back. I sat alongside her for the trip downtown. Don Hart would follow us in the radio car to Bellevue Hospital. While en route to the hospital, the girl started to complain about the handcuffs hurting her. She asked me if I could handcuff her in the front. It was against my better judgment, but she had calmed downed considerably. I agreed to cuff her in the front. I had just completed cuffing her when she grabbed my tie. She pulled my head down towards her hands and raked her long fingernails deep into my face. She would not let go of the tie and was attempting to go for my eyes. I was in an awkward position, with one knee on the floor of the ambulance. Finally, I punched her in the face to force her to release her grip on the tie.

We arrived at the hospital, and the attendant opened the rear door. Don Hart and the attendant took one look at me and said, "What the hell happened to you?"

I said, "D.H., watch this bitch. She's dangerous. One minute she is calm and the next minute she'll try to kill you.

The doctor examined the girl. They also cleaned and bandaged my face. The girl was admitted to the violent ward, and we returned to the station house. I had four deep scratches on my right cheek, which stretched from the lower part of my eye to my chin. I said to D.H., "I hope my wife believes this story because this does not look good."

About four months later, the Police Department put out a training bulletin, which read as follows:

"THE USE OF HANDCUFFS"

Once Hart and Herlihy handcuffed a failed suicide. They cuffed her wrists in front, just to be gentlemanly. Her language was very bad. Then she grabbed Herlihy by the tie and pulled until his face was next to her. She then raked her nails across his face. Four claw marks. Now Herlihy wears NYPD clip-on ties.

The day after the psycho incident, we were entering our radio car in front of the station house to begin a day tour. Out of the corner of my eye, I saw something come down from a building on the next block, between Lexington and Park Avenues. I said to D.H., "Pull up halfway down the block. I think I just saw a jumper." We went halfway down the block and sure enough, there was a woman in her nightgown. She was lying partially on the sidewalk and partially in the hedges. Her head had struck the cement, and it split open like a melon. Half of her brain was on the sidewalk. After I saw that, I knew there was no point in taking her pulse. I looked up at the building and saw a window open on the tenth floor. We entered the building.

The doorman, with his arms stretched out in a blocking stance, stopped us and said, "Where are you going officers?"

I dislike most doormen, not all of them, but most. This guy was one of them. He was the type of doorman who was under the impression he was guarding Fort Knox and police officers are under his regime. I grabbed him by his arm and took him outside to show him the dead woman. He said, "Aw, shit! Look what the hell she did to my hedges." My opinion of this mutt was right. I didn't know it at the time, but I was in for quite a day.

Still holding his arm, I said, "I can see you're all shook up about this suicide. What apartment did this lady occupy?"

He said, "She lives in apartment 10-B, but you can't go up until I announce you."

I grabbed him by his coat collar and said, "If I hear one more word out of your mouth, I will arrest you for interfering with a police investigation. I suggest you don't announce us, or I'll be back down here to put the cuffs on you."

D.H. and I entered the elevator and pushed the button for the tenth floor. We knocked on the door of apartment 10-B. A maid answered. She said, "Can I help you officers?" I asked if we could come in. She replied, "Yes, I'll show you to my lady. I just served her breakfast in the dining room." As we entered the dining room, the first thing I noticed was an open window. The maid said, "Oh my goodness. Where did she go?"

I said, "Miss, your lady jumped out the window."

The maid replied, "Oh my!"

Don Hart took notice of the breakfast on the table. He said, "She drank the prune juice. That will do it every time."

The bewildered maid replied, "Really." I just starred at the two of them.

D.H. was eyeing the two eggs, sausage, and bacon. I knew what he was thinking and immediately said, "No, D.H."

He looked at the maid and said, "I don't believe your lady is going to finish her breakfast. Would you mind?" He pointed to the dead lady's chair.

The maid said, "Oh please, Officer, sit down and eat." I looked at them thinking they needed help more than the lady who jumped out the window.

I said to D.H., "While you're eating the dead lady's breakfast, I'll be downstairs covering her up and waiting for the sergeant.

As I was leaving this inner sanctum, I heard the maid say, "Let me get you some coffee with that, Officer."

The sergeant and the morgue wagon arrived at the same time. I, and my overstuffed partner, left to resume patrol. I stopped at a deli for a much needed container of coffee. There was no way I was going to get Mr. Congeniality any coffee. A few hours later we received another call about a "possible jumper on the roof in the rear of the building of 320 East 80th Street."

I said to D.H., "What the hell is going on? Did the stock market crash or something?" We ran up five flights of stairs and pushed open the roof door. There was a woman just leaving the edge of the roof where she had been standing. I yelled, "Lady!" But she was already in flight. We ran to the edge in time to see her land in the back yard.

Don Hart looked at me and said, "Well, at least she was dressed for the occasion."

I looked down. The woman was dressed in a yellow jumpsuit. I turned to D.H. and said, "You know what? You are one sick bastard."

Another sector car had responded, and they would handle this case. We called it a day. Heartless Officer Hart and I signed off duty. It wasn't too long before I became just as callous to life as D.H. It's a sad to think, but we had to develop a thick skin in order to survive on this job.

CHAPTER ELEVEN

With all the arrests and summons Don Hart and I gave out, we spent a lot of our day tours in court. Usually we would be returning to our command with about two or three hours left to complete our shift. We were usually put on foot post for those remaining hours.

To avoid this, D.H. and I would stop by Bellevue Hospital to watch Dr. Milton Halpern, the chief medical examiner for New York, perform autopsies. We would look through a window in a door outside the autopsy room. Dr. Halpern had noticed us a number of times. Finally, because we were in uniform, he invited us to come inside. He said, "I notice you men are watching me a lot. I thought you might be interested in taking a closer look."

We thanked him for the invite and stood at a reasonable distance, so we wouldn't get in the way. On the table was a male in his thirties. His chest was held open by rib spreaders. His organs in the chest cavity were exposed, and Dr. Halpern was working on his head. He took a scalpel and made an incision from above his left ear, going around to the back of his head, and finishing at his right ear. Then he pulled the hair, which was attached to the scalp, forward toward his face. The face came off like a mask down to his chin, thus exposing nose bone, eye sockets, mouth and all red meat. I had never before seen this done. It amazed me to see that the human body could be so delicate.

He then took a hand-held electric saw with a small circular blade similar to ones that I've seen used to remove a cast from a broken arm and with precision movements, placed the blade one inch above the eye socket and sawed a 360 degree circle around the skull. Then the top of the skull came off with such ease. The entire brain was now visible. He took his hands and removed the brain. He placed it to the side of the table. He turned to us and said, "Look closely at the inside of the skull. Do you see that large crack?" We nodded our heads in acknowledgement. He told us that the crack was attributed to a fractured skull.

I asked Dr. Halpern, "If you were stranded somewhere and starving to death, what would be the best part of a human being to eat?"

Without hesitation he replied, "The heart. It would taste just like a hamburger."

I looked at him suspiciously and asked, "How would you know that?"

He motioned to us to come closer to the open chest cavity of the corpse. He said, "Put your face close to his chest." We did. He took a hot needle and injected it into the heart. Of course, we didn't question him. A small fizzle of smoke rose into the air. It smelled exactly like a hamburger being cooked on a barbeque.

It was time for us to get back to the station house. We thanked Dr. Halpern and jumped on the Iron Horse, which is what Don Hart called the Lexington Avenue train, and headed back to the precinct.

During the next year, we often stopped by to talk to Dr. Halpern and observe his work. We found him to be a dedicated and interesting man to speak with until that final day. This particular day, we entered the autopsy room. We saw a little girl, about nine or ten years old, on the table. She had long blonde hair and looked very small on that cold metal table. She could have very easily have been one of our kids. We both turned around to leave. This was one autopsy that we didn't want to see. Dr. Halpern greeted us, "Hi, Officers!"

His face wasn't that of the friendly doctor that we knew. You could tell that he was angry and something was bothering him. He was in the process of removing a large portion of her vagina and anus. I really wanted to get the hell out of there, but I asked, "Why are you cutting her like that?"

He looked at me and said, "The animal who raped and killed this beautiful little girl won't go to trial for a couple of years. I am going to preserve this tissue to show the jury how he brutally ripped, raped and murdered this child."

I looked at the anger in Dr. Halpern's face and said, "God bless you, Doctor. I don't think that we will be returning. This was a little too much, even for us."

He nodded and said, "I understand. Officers, take care." With no regrets, the only time we returned to the autopsy room was for a police investigation or identification.

Then, Don Hart went on vacation. I would have to choose someone to ride in his place. I asked John Cowie if he would like to partner up with me while D.H. was on vacation. John was only on the job a few years, but he knew the job as well as any cop in the precinct. He had a great sense of humor. He was the kind of guy anyone would like to be around.

We received a call from Central, a "possible cardiac." We responded immediately to the address of a hotel on Fifth Avenue. During this time in the police department, we were wearing black, waist-high leather jackets. We knocked on the door of the apartment. A woman with a German accent answered the door. As soon as she saw us, she put her hand over her mouth. In a muffled voice she said, "Nein! Nein! Ve must take off jackets! Ve look like de Gestapo!" I looked at her and asked if she had someone that was sick. She replied, "Ya! Ya! Myne housband is in ze bedroom, but ven he seez you he think you Gestapo! He vas in concentration camp! Take jackets und hats off!" Cowie started to take his uniform off.

I said, "Hey! We don't have time for this." I started for the bedroom, and Cowie followed behind me.

As we entered the room, we observed a man sitting on the bed with his back towards us. I walked around the bed. Facing him, I asked what was hurting. He looked up at me, grabbed the middle of his chest, and yelled, "Gestapo! Gestapo—achh!" He then keeled over onto the floor.

Cowie looked at me, with a smile on his face, and said "Good fucking job, D.H., You killed him." I knelt down on the floor and felt for a pulse. I couldn't find one. Cowie put a second call in for an ambulance. They claimed that they were backed up, and they would respond as soon as possible.

I told Cowie that we would have to tell the old lady that her husband was gone. He said, "You fucking killed him, so you tell her." He was bending over in pain, holding his stomach, and trying to prevent the outburst of laughter, which he was so desperately trying to hold in.

I walked into the living room and said to the woman, "We are waiting for the ambulance, but I think your husband has passed on." I then asked her if the hotel had a house doctor.

She said, "Ya!" I called the front desk and asked if the house doctor could come to the apartment. The desk clerk informed me that he would notify the doctor, who was having a cocktail at the bar, and have him go right up to the apartment. When I turned to the woman, she said "Tell them bring to Schnapps too." She was pouring the remaining scotch out of a bottle, so I assumed that she wanted a bottle of scotch.

I asked the desk clerk if they would send a bottle of scotch to the woman's apartment. He responded, "Gladly."

When the scotch arrived, the woman poured three drinks. She handed me two of them. I told her that we could not drink while we were on duty. She said, "Please! Myne housband vould vant dis." Cowie had come out of the bedroom. I handed him the drink and explained the woman's wishes. The doctor arrived and followed Cowie into the bedroom.

Soon, Cowie returned to the living room. He pulled me on the side and said, "The doctor is a little tipsy, but he pronounced the gentlemen dead." I went over to the woman and explained that the doctor confirmed that her husband was gone. She downed her drink and made another one.

About forty-five minutes later, the ambulance finally arrived with our friend Willie, who was a very competent attendant. Cowie showed him into the bedroom as I comforted the grieving wife. A few minutes had passed when I heard Cowie say, "D.H., can I see you for a minute?" I was in conversation with the wife and I didn't answer him. I knew that he wanted me to help lift the body onto the gurney. This wasn't going to happen, because they could accomplish that without me. Again I heard him call, "D.H., come in here!"

I excused myself and went into the bedroom. "What is it? Damn it!"

Cowie looked at me and whispered, "This man that the doctor said was dead, is alive. Willie has found a very faint pulse." I was speechless. I looked in Willie's direction and saw him kneeling on the floor administering CPR. He also had the patient on oxygen.

I thought for a minute and said, "What the hell do I tell the woman?"

Cowie broke out in a muffled, hysterical laugh and said, "I don't know. You fucking told her he was dead. You figure it out!"

I said, "You told me that the doctor pronounced him dead."

Cowie, trying to get the words out between the laughs, said, "Yeah! But remember when you called for the doctor. He was in the bar before he came up here."

I looked at him and said, "Holy shit. You mean he was drunk?" Cowie could not even answer me, because he was laughing so much. His face was as red as a beet.

Before I left the room, the patient was fully awake and mumbling something. We couldn't understand him but he was definitely alive. I went into the living room and told the woman that the ambulance attendant thinks he may have felt a faint pulse. I told her he is working on him but she is to stay in the living room. By this time, she was three sheets to the wind from all the scotch she had consumed. She waved her hand and replied, "Ya! Ya!"

I went back to the bedroom. The patient was very much alive and on the gurney, with an oxygen mask on his face. I looked at Cowie who was still holding his side from the pain of laughing. Willie and I were laughing quietly as I said, "I can't believe how I get into these fucking predicaments all the time."

After about five minutes, I went back to the living room and excitedly said, "Lady! We saved him. We got him back. Your husband is alive!"

She grabbed me around the neck and starting kissing me on the cheek. "Vundabar! Vundabar!" She ran into the bedroom. We immediately brought the patient down in the elevator. Willie transported him and his wife to the hospital.

As we entered the radio car Cowie said, "D.H., I want to ride with you all the time. You're a bundle of laughs!"

I smiled at him and said, "Fuck off, Cowie!"

The next day, there was an envelope at the station house with three names on it —Willie, Cowie and D.H. I opened it. Insidewas a card from the woman thanking us for saving her husband's life. Enclosed in the card were three crisp $50 bills. It was a shock and an embarrassment at the same time. I thought it best to leave things as they were. We told the story to some other cops, but nobody believed us. I couldn't blame them. What normal person would believe it?

CHAPTER TWELVE

For the next two weeks, Cowie and I had relatively quiet tours. John Cowie turned out to be a very good cop. I was happy with my decision to pick him as a partner in D.H.'s absence. He reminded me of D.H. in many ways, with his dry sense of humor and personality. He certainly kept me laughing most of the time.

There were nearly one hundred bars in our precinct, and we always had our share of bar fights. Cops and emergency room nurses believe in the old tale of a full moon made people crazy. We all felt this to be true.

I was of medium build and D.H. and Cowie were slightly taller than me with very broad shoulders and chests. When I would walk into a bar fight, nightstick in hand, the fight would slow down. A few paces behind me would be Don Hart or John Cowie. When the guys who were slugging it out spotted either one of them, the fighting would come to an abrupt halt. We would calm the situation down and leave saying "if we have to come back here, believe us, you will all live to regret it." Having said our "words of wisdom" we would leave.

Whenever I was leaving with D.H. after a bar fight, he would voice his favorite saying "that coo-coo juice is great, isn't it?"

Don Hart was back from vacation, and we were doing a four to twelve tour. We were sent to pick up mail from a precinct on the west side of Manhattan. A gypsy cab driver flagged us down at 71st Street and Columbus Avenue. Gypsy cabs were drivers not licensed by New York City and these drivers usually drove old Chevrolets. They would illegally pick-up fares in Harlem. He spoke in broken English and finally got across to us that a woman in his cab was about to give birth. Don Hart and I got out of the radio car. D.H. entered the driver's seat of the cab while I opened the rear door. There was a woman lying down on the rear seat, with one leg on the front seat, and one leg up by the rear window, completely spread eagle.

I leaned into the car, between her legs, and told her that an ambulance was on its way. As I did, I heard a noise that sounded like "woosh." The woman water had broken at that very moment. The tidal wave hit me directly in the face and chest. I could not believe the smell. I looked down at my uniform shirt, which had turned a different color.

Don Hart was kneeling in the front seat facing the rear and said, "Nice, D.H., very classy." I was about to say something when I saw the head of the baby start to appear. I placed my two hands underneath the head of the baby. The woman continued screaming, grunting and pushing. Before I actually knew what was going on, I was holding a well-developed baby boy covered with mucous and blood.

The woman calmed down. As exhausted as she was, she continued to grunt and push. Don Hart said, "She's pushing out the afterbirth. Let me have the baby!"

I looked at him and said, "Do I look fucking stupid. You're going to hold the baby, and you expect me to catch the bloody afterbirth."

He said, "Yeh! You're right there."

I said, "Fuck off! I'm covered in gook already."

I put the woman's legs together and said, "Lady, don't push anymore. The baby is out. The ambulance will be right here."

Police officers are not allowed to cut the umbilical cord; the baby must stay attached to the afterbirth. The rule is one cop holds the baby, and one idiot holds the afterbirth. Don Hart figured I was the latter. As these mind altering decisions were being made, much to my relief the ambulance arrived on the scene.

The ambulance attendant opened the rear door and started to take the woman out of the cab. I was directly opposite him. I was holding the baby when I saw the umbilical cord stretch to an ungodly length. I yelled to the attendant, "What the hell are you doing?" He didn't hear me because of the traffic. I had no choice except to kneel on the rear seat and follow the woman on her way out the opposite door. Still holding the baby, I edged out on my knees. I could feel the gook and slime that was on the seat being absorbed into the knees of my pants.

The attendant took the baby from me and placed the child on the mother's stomach. He then loaded them into the ambulance where they would be transported to St. Clare's Hospital. I told the attendant what I thought of him and then followed D.H. to our car.

D.H. turned to me and said, "I hope you don't think you're getting into this car smelling like that!"

I smiled and said, "D.H., if this state didn't have the death penalty, I know I would shoot you."

He replied, "Oh yeah! My wife, Joan, would come after you in a New York minute. She can't live without me." I told D.H. to find some newspaper or cardboard for me to sit on so I can get back to the station house.

Naturally, when I walked back into the precinct, everyone held their nose saying, "What the hell did you fall into?" I was walking as if I had a load of sand in my pants. I took a shower and put on a clean uniform. Then I went back on patrol with Doctor Hart.

As the sky opened up with a sudden rainstorm, we heard over the radio, "Overturned vehicle on the East River Drive and 63rd Street exit ramp." Don Hart picked up the job as we entered the East River Drive at 79th Street with our lights and sirens blaring. Sure enough, at the 63rd Street exit, a car had come off the turn too fast and was lying on its side. We blocked off the exit with the radio car. We put our raincoats on while walking towards the accident vehicle. The car was lying on the driver's side. I approached the car and saw the driver was a black man with his head out of the open window. The upper part of the car had crushed his head into the pavement.

I looked at D.H. and said, "That's a hell of a way to go."

Don Hart returned to the radio car to put a rush on the wrecker truck and to have a medical examiner respond from the morgue. I knelt down beside the man's head, looking into the car to see if there were any other occupants. All of a sudden the man opened his eyes and said, "Get this fucking car off my head!" I fell backwards on my ass. He scared the living shit out of me.

I yelled to D.H., "This guy is alive! Get any tow truck in the area to respond." Don Hart ran to the radio car to call it in. I took off my coat and placed it in a position that would prevent the rain from hitting the man's head. Almost immediately a tow truck arrived.

We all put our strength into lifting the car off the man's head, allowing him to pull his head inside of the car. We climbed onto the top of the car and opened the passenger door. We lifted him out. Remarkably, he was not hurt. He only had a few cuts and bruises on his head. He thanked us and climbed into the ambulance. They took him to Lenox Hill Hospital.

I was soaked to the bone. Don Hart looked at me, shook his head, and said, "I can't take you anyplace. Just look at yourself. You're such an embarrassment." I asked him to stop with the bullshit, and please take me back to the station house where I could change into some dry clothes. He did. There were only a few minutes left of the tour. We changed into our civilian clothes and went down to Kenny Beyers for a drink.

CHAPTER THIRTEEN

He was transferred to the Nineteenth Precinct from the 67th Precinct in Brooklyn to fill the vacancy left by Sergeant Perfect. Sergeant Jerry Walsh was his name. He had muscles that could crush you into a fine powder. He stood before the desk sergeant and informed the sergeant that he was going to tour the precinct to become familiar with it. He asked if there were any suggestions as to who he should ride with. The desk sergeant replied, "Any sector car will do. Just don't ride with Hart and Herlihy."

Sergeant Walsh asked, "How come?"

The desk sergeant said, "Don't get me wrong, they're good cops. They just bend the rules so often."

Sergeant Walsh said, "Call them in. I'll ride with them."

We received a radio call to report to the station house to pick up a sergeant who would be patrolling with us. I turned to D.H. and said, "Son of a bitch. Why us? Don't start getting him in a conversation like you usually do. Maybe he'll get bored and want to go back to the house." We pulled up and he was waiting on the station house steps. I opened the door and got out of the recorder's seat, because sergeants made the odd man ride in the back seat of the car. Then came the first surprise of many.

He said, "I'll ride in the back."

I gave him this strange look and said, "Okay, Sarge." We proceeded to go on patrol.

About twenty minutes had passed with no conversation at all. I knew this was killing D.H. because usually his mouth never stops. Finally the sergeant said, "Has the radio been busy?"

I answered with a short and curt, "No, it's been fairly quiet." I thought to myself, good job D.H.

Another ten minutes went by and the sergeant, speaking loudly said, "Are you two mutts gonna take me for a drink or what?"

I turned around smiling and said, "Do you want to start at the top and work down, or do you want to start at the bottom and work up?"

He replied, "Top shelf only!" That was the statement that eventually turned the three of us into a thirty-year-plus-friendship.

I said, "First stop is the Copa Cabana, if that's alright with you." His face lit up with a smile. We stopped at the Copa and introduced the sergeant to Carmine, the maitre d'. Carmine introduced him to Mr. Jules Podell, the owner of the Copa. We watched the floor show for a short while, then thanked Carmine and left to continue patrol. It was one of the duties of a sergeant to check on all cabaret and liquor licenses, so we took him to a few places. Joe Gleasons was on the list along with Paddy Quinns, Mr. Laffs, and we made Jager House on Lexington Avenue the last stop.

We advised the sergeant to always remember to bring his night stick whenever entering the Jager House. They always held large dance parties on weekends, and it was a hot spot for drunken fights. The shift was coming to an end. We turned the car over to our relief team. Sergeant Walsh thanked us for a nice night. I looked at D.H. and said, "Thank God, we finally got a down-to-earth boss."

It was a few days later when we received a job of a past burglary at 345 East 62nd Street. We would have to go up to an apartment and take the information for a U.F.61 report. This report would be forwarded to the detectives to investigate.

Ever since we had pulled the prank on Mike Hughes, with the snow in the car, I often reminded D.H. to make sure he locked the car when we went on a job. As we were taking the information on the burglary, I suddenly looked up at D.H. and said, "Did you lock the car?"

He said, "Yeah. What the hell are you so worried about?"

I said, "I noticed on the roll call sheet that Mike is riding with Cowie tonight. That makes two crazy guys in one car."

Don Hart said, "Don't sweat it, I know I locked the car. Besides, Mike probably forgot about the snow prank by now." I agreed.

We finished taking the report and headed downstairs to the car. Our car was parked across the street from the building. Something didn't look right. As I got closer to the car, I turned to D.H. and said, "I thought you locked the car?"

He walked around to the driver's side, and I heard him say, "Damn, I left the window open a crack. They used a wire hanger to get in."

I opened the door. There were piles of horseshit all over the front and back seats, real horseshit! It was neatly placed on the dashboard about three inches thick. I looked at D.H. and said, "Where the hell did they get horseshit in the middle of Manhattan?"

D.H. said, "There's a stable hidden under the East River Drive. That is where the Hanson cabs from Fifth Avenue keep their carriages and horses."

We went about the task of scooping the horseshit out of the car, onto the street. While we were doing this, a woman came by and said, "My God, Officers! Who would do such a thing?"

I replied, "It's the kids in the neighborhood. They have no respect for the police."

The woman shook her head as she said, "What a shame. The things you officers have to go through."

There was a brown paper bag in the trunk from a supermarket. I filled it halfway with horseshit for, let's say, "another time." I returned it to the trunk. When we got in the car, I said to D.H., "Let's go up to the 23rd Precinct and run the car through the car wash." He agreed and started the car. He put his finger on the defrost switch. I yelled, "NO!" It was too late. He flipped the switch. The defrost fan blew a ton of horseshit into our face and mouth, gagging us. We both jumped out of the car at the same time.

After we cleared our eyes and stopped coughing, I said, "That was a nice move, you dumb fuck!" We both stood there in the street laughing. We had to give them credit. Mike and Cowie had accomplished a beautiful sting.

We washed the car, but no matter how many cans of air freshener we used, we couldn't get the smell of horseshit out of the interior. For the next couple of hours, between jobs, we cruised around looking for Mike and Cowie. They had made sure to keep themselves scarce and we're nowhere to be seen.

It was time to turn the car over to our relief and sign out. The relief crew refused to take the car. They complained that it smelled like "some kind of horseshit." I said, "Hey! We bought the wrong kind of air freshener. Stop being babies about the whole thing. We stepped in dog shit and tried to do you guys a favor by freshening up the car. This is the thanks we get?"

They said, "Next time, don't do us any favors, alright!"

I went into the station house carrying my brown paper bag. I went directly to the basement where my locker was located. Augie Speers had a locker, which was two away from mine. Augie is a guy that everyone loved and respected because of his good nature. He also had a very distinctive voice. It sounded like he had a cold, and like his nose was all stuffed up.

Everyone knew that all you had to do to open Augie's locker was to hit it with the palm of your hand. This is exactly what I did, and the door swung open. I was dumping the horseshit onto the bottom shelf of his locker when I heard his voice. Augie was on his way down to the locker room. Joe Spinelli, dressing in the same aisle, was laughing at what I was doing. Joe heard Augie's voice and said, "You're caught now D.H. He's going to know that you did it."

I quickly closed the door to Augie's locker. I opened my locker and dumped the remainder of the horseshit on the floor in front of my locker. When Augie rounded the corner of the aisle, he saw me on my knees. I pretended that I was just finishing sweeping the horseshit out of my locker.

Augie smiled, as he always did. I looked up at him and said, "I don't think this is funny, Augie. Putting horseshit in my locker is not what I call funny."

Augie looked at me with the surprised look and said, "D.H., I swear I didn't do it. No kidding, it wasn't me." Augie then opened his locker and saw the horseshit. He jumped up and down. "D.H., look. They got me too. They put horseshit in my locker too!" He was so relieved to think he was off the hook.

I said, "Wow. They got the both of us." He started to clean his locker out with the brush that I so kindly gave him. Joe was in the corner holding back the laughter.

The next day while on patrol, Don Hart and I received a call from Central telling us to meet another unit at 81st Street and First Avenue. As we pulled up, I saw Augie on the sidewalk waving us down. We stopped and he came over to my window and said, "Where's my radio car? What did you do with my car?"

I laughed, "You lost your car!"

Augie was mad and said, "D.H., I know you took my car. Now stop the shit and take me to it."

At this point, I was laughing so hard I couldn't talk. The tears were rolling down my face. Don Hart asked Augie if he had left the keys in the car. Augie looked at him and now realized it wasn't us who took the car. He said, "We stopped at this pizza joint for a slice. The new guy I'm riding with left the keys in the ignition."

By now my laughter is out of control. I had to force myself to be serious. I said to him, "With all these teenagers around here, he leaves the car running."

Augie was hoping against hope that another crew was pulling a joke on him. I told him that we were the only guys that would do something like this, and it wasn't us. I said, "Augie, we have to notify the captain that your little police car was stolen." Once again, I started laughing. My sides were hurting, but I couldn't stop.

Augie said, "Oh shit! We can't tell the captain. He will crucify me. Where is he anyhow?"

I told him, "He's attending a diplomatic affair in the French Embassy. He will just love to hear this."

Augie and his young partner got into our car, and we drove to the French Embassy. I turned to Augie and said, "Do you want to go in?" He shook his head, indicating a "no." Don Hart and I got out of the car. I was attempting to control myself, as we entered the embassy. There was no way I would be able to tell the captain without laughing. I left the talking to D.H. After telling the story to the captain, we were told to put an alarm over the air with Central that a police car was stolen. He added, "Have Officer Speer in my office when I return to the precinct."

We left the embassy and got in the car with Augie. He was as pale as a ghost. D.H. told him that we had to put an alarm over the air with Central. Augie said, "Oh, shit. I'll never live this down." D.H. and I became hysterical. Nothing like this had ever happened before in our precinct. I pleaded with D.H. to let me inform Central. He reluctantly said, "Go ahead. Don't fool around."

I picked up the phone and called Central. I said, "This is the 19th Precinct. We have a RMP car number 772 stolen from the vicinity of 81st Street and First Avenue."

Central responded, "You have what?"

I repeated my message and added, "It's a New York City green and black police car with a little red bubble light on the top."

Central said, "Ten-4." Then they put the alarm out citywide. Augie was now trying to crawl under the seat. I heard some idiot tell Central that he would cover the traffic on the 79th Street transverse road and Fifth Avenue.

I picked up the telephone and said, "The bad guys have a police car, and they are listening to everything you say." With that, the radio went quiet. We dropped Augie at the station house to be with the nice Captain. We went back on patrol.

Not quite an hour later, we heard a radio car inform Central that they located the stolen RMP on the west side of Central Park. The car was intact. It was evident that teenagers had taken the car for a joy ride.

Augie got his ass chewed out and a five day loss of pay. He was happy that this day was finally over. So was I. If I laughed anymore, I'd get sick. D.H. and I went down to Kenny Beyers and told the gang the whole story.

CHAPTER FOURTEEN

April was upon us and it was nice to know that spring was just around the corner. We were told to stop at New York Hospital. There were some doctors and nurses in the emergency room who had a minor problem they wanted to discuss with us.

When we arrived, they told us that when they would get a break, they walked along the river walkway adjoining the East River and the Drive. As of late, they were not able to do this. There were men congregating and committing acts of oral sex on each other. This was taking place alongside the walkway that crossed over the East River Drive at 70th Street. We told them that we would look into this matter and try to correct the situation.

On one particular evening, we attempted to walk over the crosswalk on East River Drive. A lookout spotted us. The men calmly dispersed to the north the south direction before we could get down the ramp.

The next evening, we decided not to use the walkway. We would run across East River Drive between the breaks in traffic. The lookout would be unable to observe us until it was too late. We climbed the four-foot railing, which separated the walkway from the drive. We were able to corral about six men. Others immediately ran off when they saw us. The reason we were able to catch these men was because they were still engaged in oral sex. I had to swat the man on his knees with my nightstick to get his full attention. This caused the man standing to ejaculate on the man's face who was kneeling. We asked them all for identification. I heard the man who had been on his knees yell, "No!" I turned and saw him starting to run, not north or south on the walkway, but towards the four-foot railing that separated the walkway from the river.

I raised my nightstick in a motion to stop him, but it was too late. He grabbed the railing and dove into the treacherous black water of the East River. Don Hart and I looked over the rail and saw that he had been caught in the current. He started yelling, "Help me! Please help me! I can't swim!" He had jumped in the river at 70th Street and already the current had him at 69th Street.

I yelled to D.H., "Keep an eye on him. I'm going back to the car for a life preserver." When I reached the car, I put an alarm over the radio that I had a man in the East River at 69th Street. I grabbed the preserver along with 250 feet of rope and ran back to the 69th Street walkway. I ran along the walkway back to where we had been. I could not see Don Hart. When I got to 67th Street, I saw Don Hart's hat, winter jacket, and gun belt lying on the walkway. An avalanche of fear came over me, as I realized that Don Hart had jumped into the treacherous current of the East River to save this mutt. This is the life of a police officer, a perverted psychopath jumps into a river, knowing that he can't swim, and now D.H. is trying to save him.

From past experience, I knew that not many people survived after going into the East River at this particular spot. This spot is the area where the river approaches the 59th Street Bridge and the current is deadly. After calling D.H. several times, I finally heard a faint reply, "Over here...the preserver...over here...HURRY!"

It was pitch black and I couldn't see him. I quickly laid out the rope so it wouldn't get tangled. I threw it out into the blackness, with every bit of strength that I had to the area where I believed his voice was coming from. Every second praying, I held on to the end of the rope. If he would grab ahold of the preserver, I would definitely feel the tug. The full 250 feet of rope was out in the water with me still holding the end.

The rope became taunt, and I knew someone had the other end. I had no way of knowing whether it was D.H. or the nut case. Then I heard D.H. yell, "PULL, D.H., PULL!" I started pulling the rope. The current was fighting me because it had ahold of two bodies, which made it more difficult to retrieve them. It was like the river was telling me "they're mine and you're not getting them back." I heard sirens. I could see the flashing red lights coming towards me on the East River Drive. Knowing help was on the way, my adrenalin was pumped to keep pulling the rope.

In a split second, two motorcycle officers were by my side. I said, "It's my partner out there!"

They replied, "We've got the rope. Let go, we'll get him in." I hesitated knowing that D.H. could drown if I lost the rope.

The officer screamed, "Let go of the rope. We won't lose him!"

I let go. The two officers, struggling, were trying to pull them in and out of the river. Finally, from out of the darkness, I spotted D.H. with the psycho on his back. D.H. had one arm around him, in a life-saving position, with his other arm in the preserver. The nut case was the first to be pulled out of the water. He couldn't stop shivering. The water temperature was around 30 degrees. Don Hart came out next. When he saw the psycho, sitting on the ground with a blanket wrapped around him, he made a "move" towards him.

I stopped D.H. and said, "The newspaper people and a chief are here. Don't do anything stupid!"

Flashbulbs were going off everywhere. They wrapped Don Hart in a blanket. He was being interviewed by the chief of patrol. An ambulance took the nut case to the hospital where he would be evaluated by a psychiatrist. D.H. was taken to Lenox Hill Hospital were he was treated for exposure. I felt that D.H. should have been taken to Bellevue Hospital. He should have been seen by a psychiatrist for jumping into the river in the first place.

The next day, the front page of the Daily News had Don Hart wrapped in a blanket and an officer handing him his winter jacket and hat. The caption read, "Officer Herlihy Hands His Partner His Uniform After River Rescue." As always, the picture was not of me. A friend of ours, Phil Spruyt, who was concerned for our safety, stepped in front of me just as the photo was being taken.

On seeing the picture in the newspaper, Don Hart laughed and said, "You can't do anything right, can you?"

I smiled and said, "I should have let go of that rope."

The following month, the New York Daily News honored Don Hart with the Life Saving Award of the Year. I was proud of him, as was his whole family. I was to have the last laugh. It was only later that we found out that the area of the river where D.H. jumped in was exactly where a sewer emptied out. The water was highly polluted, and Don Hart contracted a bad case of the mumps from the polluted water.

After being out sick for a few weeks, Don Hart was back to work, and play, as usual. We received a call to investigate a bad odor coming from an apartment. We knew right away that it was another DOA. We couldn't gain entry through the apartment door, because the woman who lived in the apartment had too many locks on the door. We had to climb the fire escape to the third floor and enter through a window.

As we reached the window, I saw a heavy-set woman sitting at the window in a rocking chair, dead. I broke a small pane of glass by the window latch and released the lock. This let me open the bottom half of the window. The smell almost knocked us off the fire escape. We were on the fire escape quite a while, trying to figure out how we would get into the apartment without touching the DOA. Naturally, D.H. thought I should go first, since I was the slimmer of the two of us. The rocking chair and the woman were blocking the entire entrance to the apartment from the window. I slowly put one hand on the rear of the rocking chair and the other hand on the armrest. I put one leg over the woman, dragging my other leg very carefully in the window and onto the floor.

I noticed that the woman was wearing silk stockings tied in a knot at her knees. Many older women had this habit. Gravity had filled her stockings with her body fluid, and in the process, the stockings had become enormous. One slight touch and the stocking would burst open. Don Hart was entering the window. I yelled, "D.H., be careful. Don't touch her legs."

No sooner did the words come out of my mouth, then I saw his shoe hit the stocking on one of her legs. The fluid poured out onto the floor. D.H. was now tumbling into the room, trying to keep his balance and not slip in the body fluid. The smell was terrible to start, but now it became unbearable. We both ran for the front door. The door had four police locks and a bar going into the floor. We weren't about to get out as fast as we thought we could. It took forever to unlock them all. Soon we were in the hallway, trying to breath through our handkerchiefs.

The sergeant arrived along with the ambulance and the doctor. Soon, the medical examiner and morgue wagon were on the scene. The morgue attendants put the heavy woman in the black body bag. They told us that they had to go downstairs to get outside for some fresh air. D.H. and I said, "Go ahead. We will start to take the body down the three flights of stairs."

Don Hart and I dragged the body out to the top of the very narrow stairs. I couldn't believe the weight of this woman. We decided that both of us would stay on the top of the stairs and hold the two handles of the body bag. We would then let it slide slowly down the stairs. Not realizing the weight of this woman was too much, even for two men, we started to lift the body bag to send it on its way. The handles of the body bag came right out of our hands. The body went sliding, thumpety thump, down the flight of stairs. At that very moment, the woman who lived in the apartment at the bottom of the stairs, on the second floor, opened her door to see what all the commotion was about. The body bag went right past her, like a locomotive train, and into her apartment.

I yelled, "Holy Shit!" We ran down the stairs trying not to laugh. I turned to the woman and said, "Lady, we're very sorry. We lost our grip on the bag."

She said, "Are you officers all right! I know that woman was quite a heavy lady. Are you sure you didn't hurt yourselves?" I started laughing and assured her that we were all right. We then went to remove the body bag from her living room. Then, the morgue attendants arrived. It took the four of us the better part of a half an hour to get the body into the morgue wagon. Everyone accomplished what they had to do and then left as fast as they could.

We then went for bitters and lemon, and then headed back to the station house for a change of clothes. I was bitching and moaning to D.H. about how the police department should pay for the dry cleaning of our uniforms, especially with all the DOAs we'd been handling. He told me it would be a cold day in hell before that would happen.

CHAPTER FIFTEEN

When we become police officers, we automatically accept the danger that comes with the job. We are aware that we can be shot while walking down the street. We can walk into a holdup and be shot at any time, or be struck by a car while handling traffic at the scene of an accident. This is why when police officers leave their homes for work, they put aside any differences they might have and kiss or hug their significant others as they step out of the door. They are aware that this may be the very last time they will see their loved ones. This thought, consciously or unconsciously, is constantly on every cops mind.

When we are in the police station, we feel safe and secure. We are surrounded by other officers carrying guns. Under these circumstances, no one in their right mind would dare to harm us. At least, we felt that was the consensus of opinion.

On this particular day, Don Hart and I were on patrol. It was a fairly quiet evening. All of a sudden, over the radio came "we have a 1013 in the Nineteenth Precinct, with shots fired!" A 1013 is a code that an officer needs help. Needless to say, with a 1013 call, every available unit speeds toward the station house.

The desk lieutenant was standing on duty behind a tall desk located right in front of you as you walk in the front door. A man entered the station house and walked up to the desk. Without hesitation or reason, he pulled out a gun and fired it point blank at the lieutenant. The bullet hit the lieutenant squarely in the chest throwing him backwards onto the floor; where he then laid critically wounded. A deputy inspector, with many years on the job, was in his office located directly across from the front desk. He charged out of his office upon hearing the gunshot, and he came face to face with this deranged individual holding the gun.

Without hesitation, the deputy inspector fired his weapon three times, hitting his mark with every shot. The psycho fell dead on the station house floor. By the time D.H. and I arrived, the shooting was all over and an ambulance was en route. The lieutenant was admitted to Lenox Hill Hospital in critical condition. With his wife, who was also a police sergeant in another command, at his side, he spent the next few weeks recovering.

This unfortunate event reminded every cop just how vulnerable we become the minute we are in our uniforms and carrying our badges. From that day on, a police officer was assigned to the front of every station house in the city of New York. They were to check and identify everyone coming into a police station.

It was a cold day in November, and we were working a day tour. We were cruising along Madison Avenue, when my eye caught sight of something unusual in an art gallery. I told Don Hart to stop the car so I could have a better look. I was looking up at a second floor showroom window. Boldly displayed in the showroom window, for public viewing, was an American flag in the shape of a penis. I looked at D.H. and said, "Now that must be against the law."

We entered the gallery and asked to speak to a manager. Instead, the owner of the gallery introduced himself. We asked why the American flag was in the obvious shape of a penis. The owner replied, "That, Officers, is freedom of expression."

D.H. said, "We don't believe you are allowed to desecrate the American flag in this way. So as General MacArthur once said, 'I shall return.' And so shall we!"

We drove to the station house and spoke with Pat Burns. He was our community relations man. We described what had taken place in the art gallery, and Pat asked to be taken to the gallery. Pat Burns is one officer who knows the law inside out, top to bottom. He will not take any action unless he is sure that he is right.

Officer Burns discussed the situation with the owner of the gallery and told him that he would have to remove the object from the window. The owner flat out refused to remove the flag. Officer Burns replied, "In that case, I am going to issue you a summons for desecration of the American flag. We will see you in court." D.H. and I drove Officer Burns back to the station house and continued on patrol.

A few weeks later, we appeared in court for the trial. Pat Burns was called to the stand by the art gallery's defense attorney. During the questioning of Pat Burns, the defense attorney asked, "Officer Burns, you say this was an American flag made into the shape of a naked erect penis. Is that correct?"

Officer Burns responded, "Yes."

The defense attorney smiled, looked around the courtroom with an air of confidence and replied, "I suppose you are an authority on flags?"

Pat Burns answered, "As a matter of fact, I am an authority on flags. I was in the United States Navy aboard a destroyer ship as a signalman. I had to be able to identify the flags of all nations, large or small."

The smile of confidence came off the attorney's face as he continued with his questioning. The defense attorney once again asked Officer Burns, "You stated in your complaint that this flag was shaped in the form of a naked erect penis, is that correct?"

Pat Burns once again answered, "Yes."

The attorney stared at Officer Burns and said, "Are you going to sit there and tell me that you are also an authority on naked erect penises?"

I looked at D.H. and said, "Oh, shit. How the hell is he going to explain this one?"

Don Hart smiled and said, "I don't know, but I wouldn't leave this courtroom now for a million dollars."

Pat Burns looked at the defense attorney, who was now gloating at his audience in the courtroom, and answered, "Yes, I believe I am an authority on naked erect penises."

The attorney turned around quickly and said, "You are? And just how would explain that?"

Pat Burns looked at the judge and said, "Your Honor, I have seven children. I believe that qualifies me to know a naked erect penis when I see one."

Everyone in the courtroom quietly chuckled. D.H. and I were not going to be able to hold back the laughter much longer, so we left the courtroom. When we got outside I said to D.H., "Pat has balls of a brass monkey."

The next day all the newspapers carried the story about the American flag and Officer Pat Burns who had stood by his convictions. Pat was later recognized by veterans groups, including the American Legion, for standing behind the value and integrity of the American flag.

We returned to the station house where we were assigned a radio car to finish our tour. We were in the area of 63rd Street and Lexington Avenue when I saw a car driving with no headlights. I put the turret light on and gave the driver a short blast with the siren. He pulled over to the curb. I asked the driver, who was accompanied by a female passenger, for his driver's license and to step out of the car. The driver complied and stepped out of the car. I told him that he was driving without headlights, which is dangerous. I asked him if he thought a warning would be sufficient to send him a message about turning on headlights?

He answered, "Why aren't you out catching the real criminals?"

It was then that I smelled the alcohol on his breath. Then his female companion stepped out of the car and said, "Howard, get back in the car. Don't pay any attention to these assholes."

I looked at the woman, also intoxicated, and said, "Howard, my man, you are now under arrest for driving while intoxicated." Then, I read him his rights.

His companion asked, "Where shall I meet you so I can bail him out of jail?"

I said, "There won't be any bail because I am impounding the vehicle. You'll be taking a cab to the Nineteenth Precinct."

He was given a sobriety test by the emergency service unit. Of course, he failed the test. And, he was still belligerent and quite drunk when we took him to the precinct. The next day in court, after sobering up, he was very much a gentleman. Howard pleaded guilty and was convicted of a DWI. I thought to myself, D.H. was right. That coo-coo juice does some strange things to people. Their personalities change and they become someone even they don't like.

CHAPTER SIXTEEN

Back on the home front, we had an addition to our family. Our fifth child was born on October 29, 1970. She was a little dreamboat that we named Cathleen. My wife and I decided that five children would be enough.

Carol worked as a registered nurse in the emergency room of Mid-Island Hospital. Carol and I would work opposite shifts. This allowed one of us to be home with the kids at any given time. When it came to watching her siblings my daughter, Debbie, who was the oldest, took on a lot of responsibility. Also, Carolyn and Colleen were always there to help with Cathleen. I would be working on the house, and Debbie and Carolyn would prepare a meal while Colleen would change Cathleen's diapers. There was no question about it, we were raising five good kids!

During this time, I kept in touch with my boyhood friends as much as possible. Stewie had married and was bringing up three children. He and his family also lived on Long Island. Jerry bought a beautiful home on the ocean in South Hampton, where he lived with his wife and children. We would get together now and then for dinner and a few drinks. It wasn't as often as we would have liked, but everyone was busy with their jobs and raising their families.

My few days of being off were over. It was time to go back to the job that I truly loved. We were working a four to twelve shift, when we were told to meet a complainant. The super of an apartment house met us in the street. He explained that a tenant's sister had called and was concerned that she had not heard from her brother since yesterday. He had made it a habit to call her every morning at the same time. She became concerned when she did not hear from him. The super wanted to have the police with him when he entered the apartment, so no one could accuse him of stealing anything.

The super unlocked the door. As we entered the apartment, we saw the body of a middle aged man lying face down on the floor. He had a large knife in the center of his back. I looked at the super and said, "You're sure you didn't enter the apartment before we got here?"

He answered, "No. I'm glad that I didn't." There wasn't any odor or the presence of maggots, so we assumed that this death had occurred within the last twenty-four to forty-eight hours. Don Hart called Central and requested that the Nineteenth Squad detectives respond for a homicide. We told the super to go back to his apartment. The detectives would be talking to him later.

Jimmy Green, a first grade detective, arrived on the scene a short time later. He was accompanied by another detective, one we did not know. Jimmy was an old time detective, with twenty-plus years on the job. I can truthfully say that Jimmy was a cop when I was in diapers. He went about the crime scene in a very methodical manner: looking, kneeling by the body, touching and studying the knife, as if he wanted to pull it out of the guy and take it home.

I said to Jimmy, "We didn't touch a thing in the room. This is exactly how we found him; lying face down in front of the living room closet." Detectives have a casual way of blaming uniform cops for screwing up the crime scene. Most of the time they were right, but not this time.

Jimmy was standing in front of the closet door, his face almost kissing the door frame. For a minute, I thought he was having a stroke. He turned to me and said, "Why the hell did you call homicide? This is a suicide."

I looked at D.H. and said, "Jimmy better lay off that coo-coo juice."

I turned to Jimmy and said, "The guy has a fucking knife between his shoulder blades. I know his arms didn't reach around to his shoulder blades so he could kill himself."

Jimmy very calmly said, "Come over here kid!" He pointed to the frame of the closet where, only minutes before I had thought he was having a stroke. Then he said, "Do you see indentations in the door and the frame of the closet?"

I looked and replied, "Yeah, what about it?"

Jimmy said, "This guy put the knife between the frame and the door itself; thus, holding the door open just enough to place the knife pointing out in a straight position. He then jammed his back onto the knife letting go of the door handle. This released the knife, and he fell forward with the knife stuck in his back."

I stood there dumbfounded, my jaws almost touching the floor. Jimmy continued, "If you examine the handle of the knife, you will see that the paint chips on the handle match the paint on the door frame." My mouth was still open as Jimmy bid us a "Good night." I starred after him in amazement.

D.H. said, "That's why he gets paid the big bucks."

I said to D.H., "If I live to be one hundred; I'll never be that good!"

D.H. and I notified the medical examiner to have the body removed so we could get back on patrol. I asked D.H., "Why do you suppose that guy went to all that trouble to make it look like a murder?"

Don Hart replied, "The only thing I can think of is that he wanted someone to collect on his insurance policy. The insurance companies don't pay off on a suicide."

I stared out the window of the patrol car and thought, "The things that go on in this job will never cease to amaze me."

We stopped at Lenox Hills Hospital Emergency Room to grab a cup of coffee and bullshit with the nurses. We were standing there for a while, when a nurse came up to us and said, "Are you here to see Mike Hughes?"

D.H. and I shocked said, "Mike Hughes the cop?"

The nurse nodded yes and said, "He thought he was having a heart attack. His cardiogram came back negative. It was just an anxiety attack." She added, "If you care to talk to him, he's behind curtain two." We went behind the curtain. Mike was lying there on a gurney with his shirt off.

We asked him how he felt. He said, "The doctors think I had a heart attack." It was obvious that he had not yet received the good news. We decided not to tell him either. Because he scared the shit out of both of us, we grabbed both his hands and handcuffed them together to the rails on the bed. We took his underwear and pants off, leaving him butt naked except for his gun belt and socks. We waved goodbye as he struggled in bed. We told the young nurse that Mike wanted a cup of coffee.

She said, "I'll get it right away." We heard her screams, as the exit door was closing behind us.

When we returned to the station house at the end of the shift, we asked some guys if they had seen Mike Hughes come in yet. They told us that he was downstairs changing to go home. Don Hart immediately went to a phone and dialed the extension to the downstairs locker room.

I heard him ask for Mike Hughes. I couldn't figure out what he was up to. He then disguised his voice and said, "Mr. Hughes, this is Dr. Flavitz in Lenox Hill Emergency Room. It appears that I misread your cardiogram. You are definitely having a heart attack." He continued, "No, Mr. Hughes, I don't want you to drive. I want you to get in a taxicab as soon as possible, and meet me in the emergency room."

There was a pause and then D.H. said, "Fine, I will see you shortly." I smiled and continued down the stairs to the locker room.

The following day we were standing roll call. Mike Hughes, standing behind us, leaned over our shoulders and whispered, "I want to see you two fucks outside. You are both on a foot post and so am I." We learned that Mike had gone to the hospital and told the nurse that he was to meet with Dr. Flavitz who had called and told him he was mis-diagnosed and that he was having a heart attack.

The nurse looked at him in a peculiar manner and said, "We don't have a Dr. Flavitz on our staff. Besides, Dr. Duca told you that you were only having a slight anxiety attack. There's nothing wrong with you. Your two buddies, the D.H. s, are aware of this." Mike's eyes opened wide. He was embarrassed and raging mad. It dawned on him that the two D.H. s had gotten him again. He immediately left the hospital.

Roll call was over. D.H. and I were the first out the door and we were moving at a very fast pace. We looked over our shoulder and saw Mike Hughes trotting quickly after us. We broke into a fast run down 67th Street across Lexington Avenue towards Park Avenue. People were looking at us trying to figure out why two cops were being chased by another cop. As we were running on the sidewalk, I noticed a Con Edison truck driving down 67th Street. The side door was open. The drivers often did this so they could get a breath of fresh air. I yelled to D.H., "Jump in the Con Ed truck!" We both ran alongside the truck, making the jump inside with ease.

The driver said, "Howdy, Officers." He then continued down the street.

We both looked back out of the sliding door at Mike Hughes. He was still running when he stepped in a large pile of dog shit. Both of his feet left the ground and then he landed on his elbows. I almost wet my pants just watching him.

Later that evening, we made our usual stop at Lenox Hill Emergency Room for coffee. The same young nurse came over to us and said, "Hi, D.H., isn't it a shame the luck that Officer Hughes is having lately?" We laughed and agreed thinking that she was talking about our Dr. Flavitz joke. She said, "He came in a few hours ago complaining about pain in his elbow. He stepped in some dog shit and fell on his elbow."

We said, "Is that right?"

The nurse took out a clipboard and said, "We took an x-ray, and the doctor took a wet reading. We told Officer Hughes that his elbow was not broken. But now that the x-ray is dry, the doctor can see a break in the elbow. We can't seem to get ahold of him to tell him he must have a cast put on his arm right away. If not, it could cause more damage."

I looked at the nurse and said, "And you want us to tell him that he has to come into Lenox Hill Emergency Room because his arm is really broken?" Don Hart and I started laughing. The nurse looked completely bewildered. I said to the nurse, "There is no way in hell that Mike Hughes would believe anything we told him. It's too long a story to explain. You are going to have to figure a way to get in touch with him."

When we got back to the station house at midnight, the desk lieutenant grabbed us and said, "You guys are friends of Mike Hughes. See if you can get ahold of him. Lenox Hill Hospital wants him back there. He has a broken arm."

D.H. and I looked at each other and said, "We'll try."

We called Mike's house. His wife answered on the fourth ring. She knew us from parties we had attended together. Just as we guessed his wife said, "Don't you guy's ever quit. Mike is asleep, and I'm not going to wake him. Thank you for your concern!" She hung up the phone.

We were off for a few days. When we returned to work, Mike happened to be at the station house making out some paperwork. He came over to us with his arm in a cast. He apologized for his wife not believing our phone call and hanging up on us. He told us that the next day his arm was killing him and he went back to Lenox Hill Hospital, and they informed him of the mistake. After he left Lenox, he went to a hospital in the Bronx, where he lived, and they put his arm in a cast.

We all laughed. I said to Mike, "You can't blame your wife for not believing us after all the shit we pull around here."

Mike laughed and agreed with me. He said, "At least I'll be safe from you two guys for a while!"

CHAPTER SEVENTEEN

We received a call on a "woman having a miscarriage." She was in an apartment located in an upper-class building that had just been built on First Avenue. When we reached the apartment, we found the woman bleeding profusely after having a legal abortion. We were told by the woman's husband that a doctor in the apartment building had cut the umbilical cord while his wife sat on the toilet bowl.

We put a call in for an ambulance. We were told that there would be a delay, and we received permission to transport the woman by radio car to the hospital. I asked the husband, "Where is the fetus? We will have to bring it to the hospital."

He said, "In the toilet bowl. Where else would it be?" I just starred at this man while asking Don Hart to retrieve the dead baby from the toilet bowl. The baby was almost fully developed. I wrapped the baby in a towel and held it. We rushed them to Lenox Hill Hospital Emergency Room.

Afterwards, I was wondering why they would abort a baby that was almost fully developed. When I asked, I was told there were complications with the pregnancy, and the mother's life was in danger. Whether this was true or not, I would never find out.

A few hours later, we were handling an accident on the upper level of the 59th Street Bridge, on the Manhattan bound side. When we arrived at the scene, I positioned the police car behind the accident with the turret lights on. We had just been issued a new police car, which was equipped with turret lights that would stand straight up in the air about four feet above the roof of the police car.

A tow truck driver was lying on the ground attempting to hook a chain to one of the damaged vehicles directly in front of my car. I was positioned about fifteen feet from the tow truck driver. For a reason that I can't explain, I said to D.H., who was in the recorder's seat making out the paperwork, "I'm going to back the car up about twenty or thirty feet. I don't like being this close to the driver laying on the ground."

I did just that, and Don Hart opened his door to get some air. We were talking for awhile, and then I looked in the rear view mirror. A car was coming at us at a high rate of speed. I couldn't believe that the driver did not see the red and yellow turret lights. It was at night; it was dark; and there was no other cars on the bridge. The reflection from our turret lights was bouncing off the steel of the bridge. I yelled to D.H., "HOLD ON! We're going to get hit! This mutt doesn't see us!"

I jammed my foot as hard as I could on the brake to prevent us from crashing into the tow truck and killing the driver who was still lying on the ground. The impact of the crash to the rear of our car was horrendous. It moved our car forward about twenty-five feet. I was thrown to the floor of the passenger seat. I saw Don Hart being thrown from the car toward the railing, and the river below us. When my head cleared, I kicked open the driver's door, which had become jammed from the impact. I ran around the car yelling, "D.H.! D.H.!" I knew it was two hundred feet to the water, and no one would survive that fall into the East River. As I got to the other side of the car, I saw D.H. lying down with his back to the railing. This railing had stopped him from going over the bridge.

He stood up and said, "We had better call Central and get some more radio cars up here." The tow truck driver ran over to us. He thanked us for having the good sense to put some distance between him and our car. The ambulances arrived and transported us to Lenox Hill Hospital. We were treated and released with minor injuries. The driver of the car that hit us was given a summons for a number of violations, including failure to take due care.

Days later, I was working my last tour. D.H. had taken a personal day off. I was partnered up with Officer Fitzgerald. We were patrolling the area of 76th Street and York Avenue when we received a call from Central. A man was holding two doctors at bay with a gun in the lobby of New York Hospital. We made a quick u-turn and sped down York Avenue without the use of lights or sirens. As we arrived at the hospital, I was surprised to see a sergeant, along with two or three other police officers, already on the scene.

As we exited our car, I noticed that the sergeant and other police officers were not from our command. They said that they were passing by when they heard the call come over the air. I asked the sergeant, "What is the situation inside the hospital?"

He replied, "All I know is what Central told us. We're waiting for the Emergency Service Unit to respond." I told the sergeant that the Emergency Service Unit was located in the borough of Queens. They only had two units to cover Queens and Manhattan. It would be quite a while before they would arrive.

He was an older gentleman with gray hair. It looked to me as if he was just hanging in there for a few more years to build up his pension. I told him that I thought at least one of us should go into the hospital to see what we were up against. The sergeant looked at me and said, "I'm in charge here! No one is going anywhere until the Emergency Service Unit arrives. Do you understand that, Officer?"

I said, "Fine. Then you handle this fiasco. We're going back on patrol." I turned to Fitz and said, "Let's go. We're out of here." We departed the scene, out of view of the Sergeant. At this time, there was no such thing in the police department as hostage negotiation teams. This kind of team came about in the years to come.

Fitz said to me, "D.H., we were assigned the job from Central. We can't just walk away from it."

I told Fitz, "I'm not walking away, but as long as we stay with the sergeant, he has the rank and the power to keep us standing here with our fingers up our ass." With that having been said, we walked around to the side of the building where there was an exit door to the hospital.

Two doctors were coming out of the building. We stopped them to see if they knew anything of the situation. One doctor said, "Yes! There is a man in the lobby holding a gun on two doctors. That is why we came out this door. He can't see this door from where he is standing." I asked them to explain where the man was in relation to the door. The doctor answered, "When you go in this door, turn left. Straight down the corridor about fifty feet is a couch alongside the walkway. The man is standing in front of the couch."

I said, "It seems that everyone is going about their daily business while this man is holding a gun on two doctors."

The doctor agreed and said, "You can't tell that he has a gun. Not everyone takes notice. The staff walks by him, and the gunman doesn't even look at them." I asked both doctors if we could borrow their long white lab coats. They both agreed without hesitation. Fitz and I took off our coats and gun belts. We stuck our revolvers in our pant's belts. Handing our coats and gun belts to the doctors, I asked them to hold on to them and not leave the area. I explained to them that our police shields were still pinned to our coats.

One doctor handed me a clipboard. He said, "This will make you look more official."

As we approached the door Fitz turned to me and said, "You know that we are disobeying a direct order from the sergeant by going into the hospital? Do you have any idea what we are going to do when we get in there?"

I said, "First of all, I think if we wait like the good sergeant said, this guy may start shooting. We could have two dead doctors on our hands. We can walk together, talking loud about your golf game or anything else that comes to mind. We will size up the situation. If we can jump him without putting the doctors in danger, then that's what we'll do. If not, we will just keep walking past them and out the front door. Then we'll wait for the Emergency Service Unit with their bulletproof vests." I then added, "Above all, we don't fire our guns in the hospital. At the very least, we'll know what kind of situation we are up against."

Fitz smiled and said, "I'm with you. But even if we pull this off we will still be in deep shit."

I replied, "Hey, Isn't that what life is all about? One big bucket of shit."

We started down the corridor. I was looking at the clipboard, and Fitz was telling me about his golf game, which I knew he had never played in his life. As we approached the area where the doctors were being held, I could see the man who was holding the gun. The hand holding the gun was at his side with the barrel pointing towards the floor. The two very nervous doctors were standing in front of him. He was chastising them for some reason I didn't know. I did know he could hear us walking and talking, but he never took his eyes away from the doctors. He never once glanced in our direction. It seemed that he was oblivious to everything and everyone around him. He had his back towards us as Fitz and I walked directly behind him. There was a very large couch between the gunman and us. We knew this would be our only chance to surprise him.

I took about three giant steps and went airborne over the couch, hitting the gunman around his head and shoulder with my body. Fitz, also airborne, struck him about waist high at the same exact time. All three of us fell to the floor. I had hold of the man's hand that was holding the gun. I heard Fitz yelling, "The gun! Get the gun!"

I yelled, "I've got it! I've got the gun!" This was all happening while we were rolling on the floor with the perpetrator.

I put my knee to his neck as he lay on his stomach. Fitz cuffed his hands behind his back. We stood him up. The doctors immediately sat down and their knees were visibly shaking. I jotted down their names, and told them that they had been through enough for one day. We would contact them at a later date. We escorted the gunman out of the hospital as fast as possible, so as not to make a scene, and walked towards our car.

There stood the sergeant and the two doctors holding our uniforms. The sergeant looked, as could be expected, madder than a bulldog. He said, "I will see you two men in the station house!" We went to the station house and started processing the arrest, which Officer Fitzgerald would take for the record. As we were doing the paperwork, another officer came over to us and said, "The captain wants you two guys in his office forthwith." Knowing the word "forthwith" always meant trouble,

I looked at Fitz and said, "Here comes the bucket of shit I was telling you about."

We entered the office and stood at attention. Behind the desk stood a very distinguished looking man by the name of Captain Kelly. He looked at us for quite a while without saying a word. Visions of a police department complaint and a loss of pay immediately came to mind. He said, "Weren't you two men ordered by a sergeant not to go in the hospital, and then you blatantly disobeyed that order?"

There was a pause and I said, "I was the senior man in the car and Fitzgerald was only doing what I asked of him." The captain stood there listening. I continued, "I informed the sergeant that the Emergency Service Unit was in the Borough of Queens, and it would take some time before they would arrive. Besides, the fact that the sergeant would not let anyone go inside the hospital to size up the situation, did not make any sense to me. Two doctors lives were in the balance, and the sergeant chose to wait outside of the Hospital. It looked to me as if the Sergeant was afraid to make a decision and would rather pawn the responsibility off on another boss whenever he arrived at the scene, whenever that would be." I ended with, "And yes, sir. We take responsibility for our actions."

The captain walked around to the front of the desk and stood directly in front of us. He said, "Well, I just wanted to congratulate both of you men for doing a fine job of police work. I am putting both of you men in for a Medal of Commendation. However, between you and me, consider yourselves yelled at for disobeying a direct order." Captain Kelly then shook our hands and said, "You're dismissed."

As we exited the office Fitz said, "Wow! That's the first medal that I ever got."

I looked at him and said, "We're both lucky that we went before Captain Kelly. He is known as a "cop's cop." Anyone else would have nailed us to the cross. Kelly came up through the ranks, and from what I've heard was a hell of a hero cop himself."

We finished our paperwork, and it was off to Kenny Beyers Café. We met up with George Hardy and the guys and celebrated the good fortune of not getting a police department complaint and a loss of pay.

CHAPTER EIGHTEEN

The call came over the radio loud and clear "SHOTS FIRED—85th Street and Fifth Avenue in Central Park." Don Hart slammed down the gas pedal, and we were en-route with lights and sirens blaring. We were about the fifth car to arrive at the scene. We were told a man was on the roof of a building just inside the wall separating the Park from the Fifth Avenue sidewalk. The building contained restrooms for men and women.

We angled our car in the street and slid out the driver's door, keeping the car between us and the man shooting. I could see Phil Sheridan crouched down behind his car just a short distance from us. He motioned to keep our heads down and yelled, "This nut is shooting at anything that moves!"

I wanted to look over our car to see if I could get a shot off at the gunman, but D.H. grabbed my arm and said, "Not a good idea!"

We could hear the gunman firing shots and the sound of bullets ricocheting off objects. All of a sudden I heard Officer Sheridan yell, "I'm hit. Son of a bitch! I'm hit!"

I started to laugh and said to D.H., "How can he be hit? He's behind the car. The bullets aren't going through the cars." When I looked over at Phil, I could tell that he took a bullet somewhere in his leg.

It wasn't too long after that we heard over the police radio, "The gunman has been shot. He's dead." A cop had managed to climb onto the roof of the building, without being seen by the gunman. He was able to get a clear shot off and killed him.

Later on, we learned that Officer Sheridan was hit by a bullet, which skidded along the roadway and under his car striking him in his ankle. Sheridan was rushed to Lenox Hill Hospital. D.H. and I went back on patrol.

Later that evening we received a call asking us to "respond to the Copa Cabana, 10 East 60th Street, men fighting in front of location." As we pulled up to the location, I saw two men standing over a man lying on the sidewalk. He was lying face down with his head about one foot from the building, his feet pointing toward the roadway. I approached to check his condition. I touched his neck for a pulse. His skin was cold as ice, and there wasn't a pulse. As I was kneeling beside the victim, I looked up at the two well-dressed businessmen and asked, "What the hell happened here?"

Both men started talking at the same time. They said, "Three black men jumped us and starting beating on our friend. They tried to rob us." Each businessman would correct the other's version about what and how the incident had occurred.

Don Hart said, "Turn the victim over on his back, and look for other injuries. Maybe he was shot."

I turned the victim over and said, "Whoa!!" His face was not there. He had been beaten so badly that his face was unrecognizable. I said to D.H., "Three robbers don't take the time to do this just to rob you."

Don Hart said, "Look and see if he has some ID." As I was searching his pockets, I felt something that was in a small leather case. I pulled the case out of his pocket. When I looked at it, I almost shit. There it was, a police lieutenant's gold shield and ID card.

I looked at D.H. and said, "This guy's a cop, in fact, a lieutenant. You better get some brass over here right away."

Don Hart asked, "Does he have his off duty gun on him?"

I told him that I didn't find a gun. I was examining his I.D. card and said, "Holy shit, D.H., you're not going to believe who this is!"

From his photo ID, we knew this lieutenant. We were introduced to him at a retirement party about three weeks earlier. I remember that D.H. and I commented on what a nice guy he was. He was known as a great boss.

Don Hart put the call in for detectives to respond forthwith to our location. We started to question the friends as to exactly what had occurred. It was quite obvious they were trying to concoct a story as they were relating it to us.

Another sector car arrived. We placed both men in separate cars waiting for the detectives to show up. While examining the scene, we observed blood on the top of the curb, which was about fifteen feet away from the body. I went to the car and asked the one guy if the fight had occurred by the curb on the sidewalk.

He answered, "Yes! That's where they jumped us from behind."

I asked him, "Who moved the body back towards the building?" He looked at me and couldn't answer. The expression on his face was one of bewilderment. I went over to D.H. and said, "Let's talk to Carmine, the maitre d'. There's more to this story than these guys are telling us."

We asked the other sector car officers to watch the two men while we went inside the Copa to question Carmine. Carmine told us that all three men were friends and regulars at the lounge. He said, "They weren't drunk. They had a few drinks and started arguing among themselves as they were leaving." We told Carmine that the two guys had said they were jumped by three black men. Carmine quickly replied, "No way! They were fighting among themselves. As a matter of fact, the lieutenant and the taller gentlemen, of the two that you are detaining, were slugging it out on the sidewalk."

We left the Copa and returned to the sidewalk, awaiting the arrival of the detectives. I said to D.H., "It looks like the guy who beat the lieutenant was in a fit of frenzy and kept smashing his face against the curb."

A short time later, the crime scene was swarming with detectives and bosses. We informed everyone involved about the information we had gathered. We were dismissed from the scene to resume patrol. When the detectives notified the lieutenant's wife of his death, she immediately requested that the police department notify his best friend. She was then informed that her husband and his friend were together at the time of his death, and he was being questioned about the crime.

Whenever a cop is killed, it takes a toll on everyone wearing the uniform. You didn't have to know him or even like him. It just hits you as if you lost someone in your family. The fact of the matter is you've lost a brother officer. D.H. and I never followed up to find out the conclusion of the story. We left that up to the courts. We just wanted to forget that horrible day.

It was a few weeks later. Don Hart and I were assigned to the Macy's Day Parade on 34th Street. Due to traffic, I arrived at the station house a little late. Don Hart was waiting with a few other guys to head down to 34th Street. I told him to give me five minutes, and I would be ready to go. I quickly got in uniform, and we were on our way downtown.

As always, there were hundreds of cops milling around waiting to be assigned. One cop approached me and said, "Are you a New York City police officer?" I didn't know this cop.

I said, "What are you some kind of comedian?"

He looked at me and said, "No, but New York City cops usually carry guns!"

The words were no sooner out of his mouth when my hand slapped my holster, and it was empty! In my rush to get dressed, I'd left my gun on the shelf of my locker. I glanced at D.H. and said, "Son of a bitch. I can't walk around with an empty holster." He was laughing so hard that he couldn't answer me. A boss would definitely spot an empty holster. I was sure to get a complaint, which meant a loss of pay for a few days.

My head was turning in all directions. I had no idea what I was looking for. Then I spotted it—a five and ten cent store. I went inside and directly to the toy department. There it was, my salvation, a Lone Ranger chrome pistol with bone handle grips. I took the clear plastic box to the cashier and asked, "How much?"

She told me the price as I quickly opened the box. The cashier smiled as I put the Lone Ranger pistol in my holster. As I was leaving the store, the young cashier called out to me, "Officer, do you want some caps to go with your gun?"

I smiled back at her and said, "No, but thanks for asking."

I found D.H. about a half a block away. He told me that we were assigned together on that particular corner. He looked at my holster and said, "The gun looks real, but you better hope that a boss doesn't ask to inspect your revolver."

I said, "Great! You really know how to cheer a guy up. Just don't leave my side because the girl at the counter didn't give me any caps for the gun."

The day dragged by slowly without incident. We were finally heading back to the safety of the precinct. It was a few days before the constant ribbing stopped and everything went back to normal.

The next day we were on patrol on York Avenue. A woman standing in the street was waving her hands frantically for us to stop. She came running over to the car. "Please! Can you drive me home to Queens? I have to get my son's finger?"

I looked at her with a puzzled look as she jumped into the rear seat. I turned around and said, "We don't understand. What seems to be the trouble?" She quickly explained that her young son had severed off his finger. In her panic to get him to a hospital, she hailed a cab and forgot to take the finger with her.

Don Hart was driving. I immediately called Central for permission to go over the bridge to the Borough of Queens. After

I informed Central of the situation, permission was granted for an emergency run. I put the lights and sirens on, and off we went. I always felt comfortable when D.H. was speeding on a run. In all the years we rode together, we were never involved in an accident. Although the patrol car has the right of way at intersections, D.H. would slow down. When we had to go through a red light on a busy street, he would look both ways to make sure it was clear.

We retrieved the boy's finger, wrapped it in ice, and started back to Manhattan. We arrived at New York Hospital and informed Central of our location. We had made the round trip in a record twenty-three minutes. The doctors were able to reattach the boy's finger to his hand.

As we drove to the station house, I said to D.H., "I rushed and forgot my gun. The lady rushed and forgot her son's finger. I don't feel so bad." We both laughed knowing that in this crazy world, in some small way, we made a difference in someone's life today. The woman, not even knowing our names, would be eternally grateful to two police officers.

CHAPTER NINETEEN

The captain asked Don Hart and I if we would mind driving a few hours with a reporter from the New York Magazine. She was doing a story on "cop partners." He felt we would be perfect, since we were partners for about twelve years. We told him that we were hesitant because reporters have a way of twisting the facts around to suit the story. He said, "There is no way she can twist the facts or say anything bad about the two of you. Do it as a favor to me. I would really appreciate it."

When he put it in that light, we could not in good conscience refuse him. So we agreed. We were told that under no circumstances were we to put the reporter in any life threatening situation. "Let the other sector cars handle the dangerous jobs, and you men can roll up later."

She was a female reporter with a very nice personality. She took an interest in our families. We told her that I had five children, four girls and one boy, and Don Hart had four children, three boys and one girl. The shifts we worked were around the clock, and I had been riding with D.H. for twelve years. I added we spent more time in hours with each other than with our families. This was because of our schedules. She asked questions about the branches of the armed services we served in. We explained Don Hart had been in the Marines, and I had been in the army. We explained that both of us served in the Korean War, and we had college educations.

A call came over the air for us to handle a domestic dispute. We picked it up. The reporter came with us and saw how we played, "Good cop and bad cop." Both husband and wife were fighting. I would insist on arresting everyone involved, both the husband and the wife. Don Hart would try to calm me down. He would say he believes that the husband and wife would apologize to each other and shake hands.

I would say, "No way. We will only get a call later to come back here. We arrest them. Now!" In this way, we would get our point across to the husband and wife that they could work this out without being arrested.

The husband and wife would be so interested in watching D.H. and I argue over what course of action to take, they almost forget why they were arguing. I would let Don Hart talk me into backing down from making the arrest and walk off to the side. The husband and wife would thank Don Hart and shake his hand. I would get a dirty look. We would then leave the scene.

When we got back to the radio car the reporter said, "I can't believe how well that works. I've heard about the good cop-bad cop routine but never understood the logic."

I said, "It's like a vaudeville act; we've do it so many times, it comes natural." I told her, "If there is any violence used against either party, then it becomes absolutely necessary to make an arrest. There would be no adjudicating the matter at the scene, the courts would have to handle it."

The reporter rode with us another day. The following week the article hit the newsstand. Don Hart and I were on the front cover of New York Magazine. The title read, "Partners Till Death Do Us Part." We weren't happy with the title or the photo. It was taken through the windshield of our radio car with us sitting close together. It was our opinion that the title and photo might be interpreted that we were gay cops. This couldn't be further from the truth.

We put the magazine on the captain's desk and said, "Remember what we told you about reporters twisting the facts to suit their story?"

The captain read the article and said, "Maybe or maybe not."

We laughed and said, "What? Maybe we're gay or maybe we're not?" We all had a good laugh and we said, "No more reporters. Their not good for our image."

The following week, we were on midnight tour. At the time, we were unaware that this tour would go down in history. It would be in the form of a documentary made in German thirty-two years later. It was March 14, 1971, at 2:45 in the morning. We were flagged down by a man at Fifth Avenue and 59th Street. As we both exited the car, I noticed that the man's clothes were disheveled. His white shirt was full of dirt, as if he had been rolling on the ground. He was a tall man with a German accent. My first thought was here is a guy who owns a delicatessen on York Avenue in German Town and was mugged on Fifth Avenue.

I couldn't be more wrong. He said, "I was robbed at knifepoint by three females who fled in a yellow car." I asked him to describe the assailants, and he did. He also knew the license number and the make of the car. He told us that his assailants were prostitutes that they took his passport, his American currency, and his German marks along with German coins.

I asked for his name. He replied, "I am Josef Franz Strauss, Chief Minister of Finance and Defense of West Germany." I took all the information he could give me. I then asked Mr. Strauss if he wanted to go to the hospital, which he declined. Mr. Strauss then returned to his suite at the Hotel Plaza, which was located directly across the street from where he was assaulted.

I turned to D.H. and said, "This guy is an important diplomat. We better go to the station house and notify the desk lieutenant of what's gone down." We did just that, and the desk lieutenant notified headquarters of the incident. After finishing the paperwork and notifying the German Embassy of the assault on their diplomat, we proceeded back on patrol.

It was about an hour and a half later that we observed two females driving a yellow car matching the registration in our report. The car was north bound on Madison Avenue. We put the turret lights on and gave a blast of the siren, forcing the car to the curb. We approached the car, weapons in our hands, and ordered the occupants to step out of the car.

We told the two girls that they were under arrest. We informed them of their rights, handcuffed them, and placed them in the radio car. I drove to the station house with the two prostitutes, as Don Hart followed in the defendant's yellow car. The car was impounded for evidence. Don Hart searched the car in front of the station house. He found a large knife, German marks, and German coins.

Mr. Strauss was called at the Hotel Plaza. We requested he come to the Nineteenth Precinct to make an identification. When he arrived, Mr. Strauss made a positive ID of the two girls. He said, "That's two of the three girls that knocked me to the ground and robbed me at knifepoint, stealing my passport and money." Mr. Strauss asked about the whereabouts of the third prostitute. We told him that there were only two girls in the car. The third prostitute was probably dropped off at an unknown location with his passport and U.S. currency. Mr. Strauss returned to his hotel. We proceeded to make out the ton of paperwork necessary to process the arrest.

The paddy wagon picked up all female prisoners at the Nineteenth Precinct around 8:00 a.m. and transported them to Criminal Court. Don Hart and I arrived in court at 9:00 a.m. The prostitutes were charged with felony assault with a weapon and robbery. Their arraignment was held for sometime in the afternoon, and bail was set for a trial to be held a few months down the road.

We learned later that all charges against the prostitutes were dismissed. An article appeared in the newspaper a short time later with the headline reading, "Two Girls Freed In Undiplomatic Assault". The article was written by William Proctor.

Following is the article that appeared in the newspaper:

The persistent refusal of Franz Josef Strauss, West Germany's former minister of finance and defense, to appear as a witness here prompted a Manhattan Justice to dismiss robbery and grand larceny charges against two prostitutes.

Supreme Court Justice Myles Lane who dismissed the charges on a defense motion, called Strauss' reluctance to testify a "deplorable decision," which was tantamount to a license to commit crime in the streets.

Assistant District Attorney Bennet Gershman said he had notified the West German Consulate here numerous times that "it's impossible under our law to try a case without affording an accused the opportunity to confront his accuser."

But he was informed that "pressing political business in Germany" prevented Strauss now the opposition leader for the Christian Socialist Party, from attending the trial. "We also made efforts through the U.S. State Department to secure his attendance but to no avail," Gershman said.

"It's ironic in these days when crime in the streets is a burning issue that a witness -- a high official of a foreign country -- refuses to testify," Lane declared.

"In addition to negating law-enforcement work, this is a poor example to ordinary citizens."

The robbery and grand larceny charges against the prostitutes stemmed from an attack on Strauss in the early morning hours last March near the Hotel Plaza.

Three women pulled and dragged him toward a car, then pushed him down on the sidewalk and lifted his wallet before making their escape, police said.

"In my opinion the evidence would have proven the defendants guilty," Gershman declared in court.

"The police in this city devote great efforts in protecting foreign political officials, and the defendants in the case were apprehended by quick efficient police

action." Gershman added, "I hope this case doesn't mean it's going to be open season on diplomats."

Now, thirty-two years later, I was being contacted by a German television studio. They informed me that they would like to make a documentary about the events of that day. Both Don Hart and I agreed to participate. We were flown from Florida where we were living at the time, to New York City, and made the documentary in the Nineteenth Precinct, where the assault on Mr. Strauss occurred. It was aired on German television in November of 2003.

CHAPTER TWENTY

The Knapp Commission, led by a man named Whitman Knapp, was created to investigate corruption in all areas of the police department. This was at a time when a detective by the name of Serpico was in the headlines of every newspaper. The Commission had been investigating for two years, and all proceedings were held on television. It was true that the Commission arrested a lot of bad apples in the police department. It became obvious to us that this was long overdue. The problem the street cop came upon was when the Commission ran out of bad apples, they went after cops who would have a cup of coffee off his post. They would blow this up and turn it into a major violation. Something that was a minor infraction of the rules was now construed as corruption.

Cops were being harassed on a constant basis. This brought the morale of the department to an all time low. The Nineteenth Precinct was a close-knit and cheerful house. Lately, you didn't see an officer with a smile on his face. It wasn't because they were doing anything wrong. We just didn't trust our fellow officers. Some officers worked for the Knapp Commission or Internal Affairs. They were placed in precincts to collect information of all sorts. They were called "field associates." If an officer spoke to another officer not knowing he was a field associate, he might confide in the field associate that he was falling behind on his household bills. This information was then passed on to Internal Affairs. This officer would now be marked as a "potential risk to take graft."

The Knapp Commission had its fanfare on television. Politicians stuck out their chests and pinned a rose in their noses. Now Internal Affairs would pick up the reins and be the driving force. They were known as "Internal Affairs Division" or for short, IAD. Years later, they changed the name to Internal Affairs Bureau or IAB.

Internal Affairs is a necessary evil in every police department. They root out bad cops. This is a blessing to the integrity of the police department. If we were going to be "New York's Finest," then be the "Finest." Getting rid of the corrupt cops was the job of IAD.

We were no longer allowed to stop in and say hello to a store owner in our sector. We were no longer allowed to eat a sandwich with a container of coffee in your car for your meal. We must now put the car out of service and return to the station house to take our meal. We would waste an hour of time in the station house for a meal we most likely didn't even want. Don Hart and I were in the habit of stopping at a deli and grabbing a sandwich. We would eat in our car out of view of the public eye. When a call came over from Central and we were in the middle of eating, the sandwich and drink went into the trashcan. We would be on our way to answer the call. This was no longer the way things would be done. Don Hart and I were no longer the happy and fun cops that we used to be. The following incidents would conclude our days in uniform and the work we loved so much.

We were working an evening tour in Sector "A," which covered the Copa Cabana nightclub. Tom Jones was appearing on this particular day. The crowd of people waiting in line extended around the block. It was around 6 p.m. when a call came over the radio to respond to the Copa to investigate a "man with a gun." As we pulled in front of the Copa, the doorman approached our car. He told us that a man waiting in line had a gun in his belt. He told us exactly where he was waiting in line. It was my practice to drop a bullet to the bottom of my holster when going on a run where there was a weapon involved. This prevented my weapon from being locked by the leather lock that would hold my gun in place. My weapon rode free and could be removed from the holster without fear of being hampered by the leather lock.

Don Hart and I approached the man with our hands on our guns, very aware of his hand movement. The gun was visible and was right above his belt buckle. I said, "You better have a carry permit for that gun or tell me that you're on the job."

He immediately put his hands in the air and said, "I'm on the job." We told him to reach in his pocket slowly, and bring out his shield and ID card. He produced a Long Island Railroad police shield with a picture ID. At that point, I recalled reading in the newspaper, that Long Island Railroad police were issued guns the day before.

We explained to him how dangerous it was to show his weapon in that manner. I said, "A police officer in uniform, as well as the public, has no idea who you are. You put yourself and the people around you in jeopardy." We told him to slide his holster around to his side hip, where it wouldn't be visible.

As we left the area, I said to D.H., "He has a new toy. He wants everyone to see that he can carry a gun, whereas Joe Citizen can't."

Don Hart said, "He won't live long doing that!"

About an hour later, we received another call to return to the Copa to investigate an assault. As D.H. drove, I said, "I wonder if that railroad cop is involved in this assault." Upon entering the Copa, we were told that a patron was assaulted downstairs in the nightclub area. We went downstairs to the crowded nightclub floor, and sure enough, there was the railroad cop holding a cloth napkin to his head.

We asked him what had happened. He said, "One of the red coats hit me on the head with something." His reference to the "red coat" meant a supervisor of the nightclub floor. There was about a dozen of these men who wore red sports jackets. They were in charge of the waiters and the seating of the patrons. Don Hart asked the maitre d' to have all of his men wearing red coats to go into the men's restroom, where we were taking the aided railroad cop. It would be impossible to conduct an investigation in a room where Tom Jones was performing. As crude as it was, this was the only quiet place in the immediate area of the assault. The men's room was quite large. I told D.H. to take everyone to the rear of the room, and I would keep curious patrons from interfering with his investigation.

After his investigation, Don Hart told me that the aided cop could not identify any of the floor supervisors as his assailant. I asked the maitre d' if all the so-called red coats were in the men's room. He replied, "Yes." We suggested to the injured cop that we drive him to Lenox Hill Hospital to be seen by a doctor for the cut on his head. He agreed. We drove him and his wife to the hospital where he received medical attention. We returned to the station house, made out the proper paperwork, and returned to our patrol.

A few days later, we were told to report to Internal Affairs Department, housed in Brooklyn at the time, to be questioned regarding our actions the night of the assault. I looked at D.H. and said, "Now what the hell did we do wrong? What do those mutts want to question us for?" We knew that police officers never allowed Internal Affairs to question us without being represented by a PBA officer. We contacted Pat Burns immediately. As always, he was right by our side.

Don Hart and I had never before been interrogated by Internal Affairs. We were not looking forward to this ordeal. When we were in Korea, we were taught that in the event of capture by the North Koreans, you were only to give your name, rank and serial number. If we were tortured, we were to give false information.

The street cops looked at Internal Affairs as the "Nazi Gestapo" of the police department. This name fit like a glove. The only difference between the two was IAD could not torture you for information. At least, not physically; but mentally they were experts if you allowed them to get into your head.

I was the first one to be called. I was to be interrogated by four officers from the rank of captain on down to sergeant. Before I went in, I told Don Hart that his explanation of events would be the only one that they would get. I was mute, dumb, and blind. I knew that their game was to get two stories and twist both stories to suit their benefit, whatever that was.

When I first walked into the inner sanctum, they dramatically made a production of turning on a tape recorder, moving slowly as if they were in a Broadway show. "State your name, shield number and precinct where you work." I did exactly as they ordered. "Now tell us what was said when the floor men were questioned."

I smiled to myself and said, "I don't know. My partner conducted the investigation."

The captain stared at me and said, "Well what the hell were you doing?"

I replied, "I was by the entrance door to the men's room making sure that anyone who came in urinated and left when he was done."

If looks could kill, I would have been dead at that very moment. "You mean to tell this inquiry board that while a police investigation was going on, you were in charge of the urinals?"

I stared right at him with the dumbest look that I could conjure up and said, "Well I guess you could put it that way."

He slammed his hand down on the table and said, "Get out of here right now!'

I was being escorted out of the office as Don Hart was entering. Of course, I couldn't talk to him. About a half an hour later, Don Hart and Pat Burns came out of the office. D.H. and I headed back to the precinct. He told me that he told them all the details he had taken down in his memo book pertaining to the investigation of the night in question.

D.H. said that one of the issues that bothered them was the fact that we drove the aided railroad cop and his wife to the hospital in our radio car. Don Hart said that he explained to them that since the railroad cop was a law enforcement officer, we were treating him with same courtesy that we would expect if the situation were reversed.

A few days had gone by when we were called down to the PBA. office on West Broadway to confer with a lawyer. Both of us were bewildered and could not understand why we needed a lawyer. Pat Burns again accompanied us. I will never forget this dreadful day.

The lawyer read from a legal document stating that Don Hart and I were being charged with:

1. Allowing and permitting a prisoner to escape.

2. Don Herlihy was also being charged with putting a gun to the victim's head and threatening to blow his head off.

I was speechless. I looked at Don Hart who was still listening to the lawyer. His words were going through me like a spear. "These charges, if you're convicted in a court of law, carry a sentence of seven years in prison for each of you."

He was finished. I just stared at him. Then Don Hart angrily said, "Are we all on the same page? Where in the hell did all of this come from?"

I leaned against the large window in his office and waited for the lawyer's answer. "These are the findings of the Internal Affairs Division."

I interjected, "Findings! They couldn't find their ass in a closet!"

The lawyer looked at me and said, "Nice. Should I use that as a defense?"

Don Hart and I spoke to each other and then asked the lawyer, "Where are these allegations coming from?"

The lawyer replied, "Internal Affairs. They received the complaint from the railroad cop." I glanced over to Pat Burns. He looked very concerned that two of his boys were in some serious trouble. Don Hart and I quietly chatted, and then Don Hart spoke up, "You set up a photo line-up with our pictures and pictures of other cops who were not involved. Let's see if the railroad cop picks us out as the cops that put a gun to his head and let a prisoner escape."

The lawyer looked at both of us and said, "If that's what you want done, I will get on it right away. I'll be in touch with Pat Burns." With that, we left his office and went to Donohue's Bar for lunch and a cold drink.

The next few days were hell for both of us. Not knowing what Internal Affairs had in their minds as to how they would fuck us. As I said before, IAD could mentally destroy an innocent person, and they were doing just that to us.

The lawyer got in touch with Pat Burns and told him a photo lineup was conducted by Internal Affairs with him present. The railroad cop viewed our photos and said, "These are the two cops who deserve a medal for the way they handled my injuries."

Internal Affairs quickly stated, "You mean to tell us that these two cops did not put a gun to your head and allow a prisoner to escape?"

The railroad cop stated, "Hell no. These guys treated me like a gentlemen."

All charges were dropped against us. As you can guess, no apology for putting us through hell was ever forthcoming from Internal Affairs.

A short while later, D.H. and I sat in Kenny Beyers Café and had a few drinks. Both of us knew what had to be done. After fourteen years of riding together in a radio car, we had decided to go to "plainclothes." We knew this would most likely split us up as a team, and the decision made us sick. It would be like losing a brother or getting a divorce. We knew that we must give up the uniform and the work that meant so much to us.

D.H. went into the Nineteenth Precinct Anti-Crime. I followed about two weeks later. It was a plainclothes unit, and the arrests were mostly for low level crimes. I knew right away that this type of police work was not for me. God, how I missed being in uniform.

A few months went by, and I received a call from Sergeant Jerry Walsh. He was now a lieutenant commander in charge of the Organized Crime Control Bureau with Brooklyn South Narcotics. He asked me if I would be interested in working in Narcotics with Organized Crime. I hesitated and told him that I didn't like the fact that if my unknown partner took money or narcotics, they would lock up both of us. Jerry told me that can't happen the way OCCB was set up. He explained that there were modules of five men and a sergeant. Each man had a different amount of time on the job. No one man could ever convince four others and a sergeant to do any illegal act. It just wasn't a possibility that this many people could be corrupted at once. I liked that idea. I told him I would have to talk it over with D.H. At that very moment, he said, "I would love to have both of you guys working for me if it's agreeable to you."

I presented Jerry's offer to Don Hart. He said that he enjoyed Anti-Crime and was going to stay in the Nineteenth Precinct. I said, "If it's okay with you, I would like to give OCCB a try." We met that night for a couple of drinks. It was a sad night for both of us, knowing that we would never be working together again.

CHAPTER TWENTY-ONE

I was sent to the Police Academy to attend a three-week Criminal Investigation Course on narcotics. Upon completion, Lieutenant Walsh made a few phone calls and had me assigned to Brooklyn South Narcotics Division OCCB (Organized Crime Control Bureau).

Lieutenant Walsh introduced me to the men I would be teaming up with—Jimmy O'Neil, Al Brough, Kiernan Sheehan, Al Kennedy, Frankie Shields and Sergeant Jack McGovern. The names read like a map of Ireland. After being in the Nineteenth Precinct for fourteen years, around the same men for that amount of time, I thought the transition would be difficult. I couldn't have been more wrong. I was welcomed with open arms by my new team. This I welcomed as it made for happy working conditions.

My first assignment was to man a wiretap with a detective by the name of Ray Smith. Detective Smith would be in charge of the tap. The wiretap was on a well-known organized crime soldier, whose name is to be left in anonymity, as will the organized crime family he was associated with at that time. For arguments sake, we will call him "Bulldog," and he was a soldier in his "Family."

The wiretap was located in a basement of an unoccupied school. The school was located in the middle of Bedford Stuyvesant near Troop Avenue in Brooklyn. This area was predominantly black. Our only option was to enter and leave the school at night. If the neighborhood observed a white person on the block, they would immediately assume that he was a cop. The wire was manned around the clock. In order to keep the traffic of cops in and out of the school down to a minimum, we were sometimes asked to sleep over.

As you can imagine, the basement of the school was quite large. The team had done their best to make it as comfortable as possible. There were a few cots, a beach cooler for drinks, a rotisserie for cooking, and of course, a load of police telephone recording equipment. Every word that was spoken on the telephone tap would have to be transcribed into writing for the district attorney. This was an enormous task for every officer involved. Because the wiretap would get renewed every thirty days, it would encompass volumes upon volumes of handwritten transcription for the courts. If the subject was thinking as he was talking and said, "Er, er, hmm, I don't know." Those exact words and sounds would have to somehow be transcribed into writing.

I would sometimes have to call my wife to tell her that I had to sleep over at the school. This would be the result of a stakeout based on information that we received on the wiretap. She found this hard to believe. Carol was used to my coming home when my tour was finished. Carol said she did not bargain for this kind of life. I could understand her feelings, but I knew that this new job that I chose was meant for me. Naturally, in the seven years that would follow, my dedication to Organized Crime Narcotics, put a terrible strain on our marriage. It eventually led to divorce.

After a week or so of wiretap duty, I would return to the office for a break. This particular day, as I entered the Brooklyn South office, I saw a thin man squatting Indian style on top of a desk. His long hair was halfway down his back. He had a long salt and pepper beard, ending in the middle of his chest. He definitely looked like a long lost Indian from the past. I wondered why the hell this prisoner is being allowed to sit on top of a desk and no one is paying any attention to him.

I asked Lieutenant Walsh, "Why is that guy perched on top of the desk?" He smiled and said, "Let me introduce you to the undercover detective who will be working on your team's case." He took me by the arm and introduced me to "Neil." Neil and I would, in the future, become very close. I think he heard about the stunts I had pulled when I was in the Nineteenth Precinct and he thought I was a bit crazy. I thought he was crazy too for doing such dangerous work as an undercover.

I came to notice that the men in narcotics did not socialize with the families as did men in the Nineteenth Precinct. They felt that they were your family. Your mind must be on protecting each other. After a while, I understood what they meant. I quickly realized that this elite unit was not the place for any jokes or pranks. These men placed themselves in life or death situations every day.

We were asked to give extra backup to another team on a narcotics buy. This would put our Bulldog case on hold. The undercover being used, I will call "Anthony." He would be making a buy of cocaine. It would probably be a quick in and out deal.

Anthony had been recruited right out of the police academy when his training was completed. This was a common practice used by the department. This ensured that no one would know that this man was a cop. Anthony was in his mid-twenties and he had about three years on the job. As they say in the street, he could "walk the walk and talk the talk." He was perfect for work as an undercover.

The plan was for Anthony to go into a predetermined old apartment house. He would be carrying a small paper bag with the buy money. He'd make the buy and leave with the drugs. He was wired with a Kell recording device. This allowed all of his backup team to hear every word that he and the subject spoke.

We were set up in a few cars about a block away. I could hear Anthony saying, "I'm in the elevator, just passed the second floor. I'm going to get out on the third." I could hear the old elevator doors slowly open. Anthony's leather heels of his shoes could be heard on the marble floor. At the far end of the dimly lit hall, Anthony saw a man pointing a revolver, with an extra long barrel, at him. Then we heard Anthony say, "Hey! What's with the gun? There's no reason for that!"

Over the radio, his team yelled, "GO! GO! GO! IT'S A RIP OFF!"

Without hesitation, we headed for the location. It was then that I heard the shot, "WaWhamm." Then a second shot, "WaWhamm" and a third, "Wawhamm." The shots were echoing through the long hallway. Precious seconds were flying by as we sped toward the scene. We heard Anthony's laboring grunts as he tried to get down the flight of stairs to the street.

His team was first on set. Anthony was on top of the cement stoop of the apartment house. His hand was in the air as he fired two shots from a derringer pistol that he carried. He collapsed at the top of the stairs. His team was screaming into the radio, "Central! We have a 1013—cop shot! We have a cop down! We need an ambulance!"

Another team was giving the location to Central. One of his close friends on his team, Mike, held Anthony's head and was screaming, "Don't you die on me! Do you hear me? Anthony don't you die! Stay awake! Don't go to sleep!"

Minutes later, Anthony was being taken to the nearest hospital. Sirens were blasting. His team had located and arrested the shooter and all of the subjects associated with the buy. Anthony had been shot in the chest and placed in critical condition in the Intensive Care Unit. It was later we learned that when Anthony exited the elevator he saw the subject with the gun. The subject fired his first shot from a weapon that looked like a long barreled gun, which was a gun like Wyatt Earp would have carried in the western days. The first shot was high and embedded the far wall down the hall. The second found its mark and smashed into Anthony's chest. He was sent backwards onto the floor by the force of the bullet, and left staring at the ceiling. The shooter approached him, stood directly over him, and pointed the gun at Anthony's face. He fired point blank at Anthony's head and he missed! The bullet struck the marble floor close to Anthony's ear, sending chips of marble into his head. Blood was drizzled onto the floor from this injury.

Anthony played dead as the shooter grabbed the paper bag containing the buy money. He even took the time to remove Anthony's watch from his wrist. Little did the shooter know that in a matter of minutes, he would face the wrath of Anthony's team who were quickly descending upon him. It would be a year or more before he and his accomplices would go to trial for attempted murder of a police officer and numerous drug charges. All the officers of OCCB felt that no matter what the amount of prison time the court imposed on them, it would not be enough. After a year of recovering, Anthony came back to work on "light duty." Shortly thereafter, he was forced to retire on a disability because of the wounds he received that horrible night.

The object of buying drugs from a low level source was that it would give you leverage. When you would finally arrest the subject, he was given a few choices. His sentence, whatever it might be, could be lowered considerably by the district attorney. He would have to give them his supplier and more of the mutts pushing the drugs in the street. He would be registered as a confidential informant (CI) and receive a CI Number. This procedure, if he was lucky, could lead the detective investigator up the ladder.

It would lead the investigator to a so-called soldier and on up to a capo of an organized crime family, both of whom were high ranking in a crime family. Choice number two, if he didn't cooperate, was to keep his mouth shut and be sent to prison for a very long time. This time would be determined by the weight in drugs that he sold. Most choose door number one and would become an informant in order to get a reduced sentence. If their information was not good, they immediately inherited door number two.

Sergeant McGovern informed our team that we were to conduct a "Buy and Bust" operation in the Ninth Precinct in Manhattan. This was not one of our favorite things to do. It meant dropping whatever case you were working on, and doing the "Buy and Bust" operation. The positive possibility was that there was always a chance that you would get a good informant out of the operation.

Sergeant McGovern and the Lieutenant would meet us in Ryan's Bar, located around the corner from our office in Brooklyn. This is where we would discuss the layout and plan of operation. Ryan's Bar was a small neighborhood pub that catered to mailmen, sanitation men, and construction workers. Ryan was known to have the best roast beef sandwiches in town. And if you so desired, there were hard-boiled eggs and pickled pigs knuckles behind the bar. Not many women frequented this bar. There was a long regulation shuffleboard against the wall at which Frankie Shields and I became proficient at playing. There were a few tables at the rear of the bar covered with red and white-checkered table cloths. This is where we would sit with the lieutenant and the sergeant to discuss how the operation would be run.

The owner, John Ryan, was one of the nicest guys we would ever know. If we were short of money, John would lend us whatever we needed. Come payday, we would be right there to pay him back. Frankie and I would stop in for a beer. Looking at our sad faces, John would know that we were a little short of money. He would always ask, "You guys need some money until payday?"

The answer would always be, "Yeah! If it's okay with you." He knew how to bring a smile back onto our faces.

"Shuffleboard anyone?" Frankie would yell out. "Horse collars the game—me and D.H. will be partners." Frankie would then salt down the board and yell, "Let's have some quiet in here. I'm about to shoot my first puck." The whole bar would break out into laughter as his first puck went right off the end of the board.

CHAPTER TWENTY-TWO

Howie had made three or four buys that night. A few guys on the team were bringing the perpetrators into the station house for detention. I was waiting with Howie in his car for their return, so we could get at least two more subjects and call it a night. At this time in my career, I had grown a mustache and full beard. Whenever we went on a buy operation, I wore dungarees and a shag coat. Howie was staring at me in the car. I looked at him and said, "What the hell are you smiling at?"

He said, "D.H., you could make a buy. I'll tell you how to act and what to say. No shit. You can pull it off."

I said, "Sure! Walsh and McGovern would have my ass for dinner."

Howie looked out the car window and said, "You see that guy standing over there? He sells brown rock heroin. I bought off him before. Just act drunk and ask him for a couple of tins. You can pull it off." Howie was laughing as I was thinking about it. Howie picked up the radio and told the sergeant that Herlihy was going to make a buy.

The sergeant responded, "No way! He doesn't know what the hell he's doing. He'll fuck things up and burn the set."

I got out of the car without the subject spotting me. I staggered up to him and said, "Hey man, you got any shit, any brown?"

Before I could finish the sentence, the subject said, "Cool it! The man is all over here." I was staggering and swaying as he reached in his pocket. He gave me three tins, which are small squares of tin foil containing brown rock heroin. I gave him $60 and turned around the corner.

Howie informed the lieutenant and the sergeant that the buy went down, and they arrested the subject. The pusher was screaming, "No way. I didn't sell to an undercover cop. No way." At that moment, I came from around the corner. The subject saw me and said, "You're a cop? Man, you are one fucked-up dude." We all laughed and put the cuffs on him.

Walsh and McGovern were still laughing and said, "Good job, D.H."

The prisoner was taken to Central Booking and Lodging, and I went with Howie to turn in the narcotic evidence at the lab. We were finished with the tour, and it was back to Ryan's Bar for a few beers. None of the cops from the office could believe that I had made a buy. For that fact, neither did I.

The next day I entered the office and saw a message written on the blackboard, which read, "Don't anyone buy coffee. Herlihy bought enough for the week." Everyone was laughing but me. I couldn't understand what the joke was all about at the time.

Lieutenant Walsh came over to me and said, "Call the lab. They want to talk to you." I grabbed the phone and dialed the lab.

I was told to release my prisoner. "You bought Maxwell House freeze-dried coffee!" Even I had to laugh.

I released the prisoner from the holding cell. I said to him, "You sell this kind of shit to a junkie and you'll wind up dead." He just smiled and left to go back to his street sales. That was the end of my undercover career. I would stick to being an investigator.

One of the subjects that we arrested earlier that night had stated that he wanted to talk to me about something. Al Brough and myself went down to the holding pen and spoke with the subject. He said, "If I give you a Blue Coat, can I get consideration on my arrest?"

I said, "It's up to the D.A., and what the hell is a Blue Coat?"

He responded, "You know, one of you guys in uniform."

I said, "You know a cop that sells drugs?"

He said, "Hell yeah. He sells to me."

We immediately went back to the office and notified Lieutenant Walsh. He, in turn, notified IAD. We questioned the subject again with Lieutenant Walsh and IAD present at the meeting. The subject went on to tell us that the cop worked in the Thirteenth Precinct as a clerical man. He agreed to be wired with a recording device. He would go into the Thirteenth Precinct with the soul purpose of getting the cop in a conversation.

He was told to use the word "heroin" when he spoke about the drug and not the street word "horse." He would agree to this only if the drug sale he was arrested for would be squashed. IAD assured him that they would take care of it.

I was in a car, set up with recording devices, with an IAD lieutenant and a detective. We were parked about a block away from the station house. The subject sashayed into the station house as if he owned it. We heard him address the cop by name. He told him that the heroin he sold him was bad, and he would have to make good on the deal. The cop excitedly said, "I gave you good stuff, and I told you never to come to this station house. Get the hell out of here, and I will meet you later."

The subject left the station house and headed to our car. I looked at the lieutenant and the detective. I could have sworn that I saw them drooling. Every word of the conversation was on tape and as clear as a bell. My job was done. IAD would arrest the cop in their own good time. That was fine with me. I wasn't feeling too good about myself. I called Patty Burns to have a beer with him at Donahue's Bar. Patty met with me, and I told him the whole story. He looked at me and said, "You didn't lock up a cop!"

I said, "What part of this story didn't you understand?"

He said, "You locked up a drug dealer who is wearing 'our' uniform."

I smiled at him and said, "I knew that I would feel better after talking to you. Love you, Patty Burns." We both had a bite to eat and a couple of beers, and then headed home.

It was months later when Al Brough and myself had business in the Thirteenth Precinct. As we walked in, Al whispered to me "Look who is working at the desk."

There was the cop that IAD locked up months earlier. I said, "Son of a bitch. IAD probably worked out a deal with that mutt to turn in good cops for minor infractions."

We asked to speak to a PBA delegate. We pointed out the cop to him and told him that IAD locked that guy up for drugs months ago. We left the station house, cursing IAD's motives. The PBA delegate would take care of it from there. With all of the bullshit from the "Buy and Bust" out of the way, it was time to get together with the detectives left on the wiretap and catch up on Bulldog's movements.

The lieutenant informed us that Bulldog had flown to Florida and was bringing back a couple of keys of heroin. The information they received on the wire, as he spoke to his wife at the bar they owned, was that Bulldog would be arriving at Kennedy Airport that afternoon.

We imagined that he would be bringing back with him either heroin or cocaine. It was decided by the brass downtown to leave him alone. They wanted to wait in order to build a foolproof case against him, and follow the drugs to wherever they would lead us. You could almost say we woke up with him and put him to bed every night. Everywhere that he went, we went. The car he drove had a locating device on it. If he went into a restaurant to eat, one of us would be there. If he went into his social club, Neil was there. Neil was such a great undercover that Bulldog treated and loved him as a friend.

On one occasion when I was following Bulldog, he and his wife, Cleo, entered a steak house in Brooklyn. They were known to frequent the place often. It was a rather large restaurant with a long bar located at the front. Bulldog and his wife were escorted to a table in the rear. I positioned myself at the end of the bar, close to the front door, and ordered a drink. They dined for about two and a half hours before they finally got up to leave. I had just ordered another drink from the bartender.

I expected Bulldog and his wife to walk right out the front door but they stopped at the bar for a nightcap. The bartender was in the process of making my drink when he saw them standing directly in front of him. It was obvious that the bartender knew him. He put my drink on the side and addressed him by name. They were standing about six feet away from me. I was at the end turn of the bar, and Bulldog was at the straight part of the bar. His eyes were taking in everyone at the bar as he ordered his drink.

I knew he had a memory like an elephant. He wasn't one to forget a face. I was burned as far as ever being in his sight again. I said in a loud voice, "Bartender! I believe I ordered my drink before that gentlemen." The bartender looked at me, and so did Bulldog who motioned with his head for the bartender to serve me. The bartender slammed my drink on the bar in front of me, as if to say this will be your last drink served here.

I lit up a cigarette and said, "Thank you." Bulldog finished his drink and gave me that last dirty look as he left the bar. I returned to the office to make out my D.D.5, which is a case report on observations, and called it a day. I would finally be going home earlier than usual. Bulldog's case always received priority, but the team still had to work on their other cases.

We were going out to pick up a subject that we were into for a few buys. He had been out there for a few months. The lieutenant said to meet at Ryan's Bar to go over the plans on hitting the apartment. I was assigned to the sledgehammer, which would take down the apartment door. Another officer was assigned the double-barreled shotgun. I was told that door would be difficult to take down. They told me to be prepared to hit it a few times.

The procedure was for me to take the door down with the sledgehammer and immediately step out of the way, so the officer with the double-barreled shotgun would be first into the apartment. Everyone knew their assignment and post. We entered the building with no trouble and were in front of the apartment door. The order was given that everyone was in place and to hit the door. I swung the sledgehammer as hard as I could, and the door fell off its hinges. The momentum of my swing sent me forward into the apartment first. The door was not as strong as reported.

This spontaneous and unexpected movement when the door came down on the first shot placed me in front of the officer with the shotgun. I had run about four steps into the long and fairly narrow hallway, when I heard the blast from the shotgun behind me. My pants leg blew out like a balloon, and I went down on one knee. I worked my way into an alcove as the team ran past me to make the arrest of the subjects in the apartment.

I put my hand down the rear of my pants to feel where I had been hit. There was no blood. I picked up my pant legs to look at my ankles. Again, no blood. There was a large hole in the floor where I had been running. A sigh of relief swept over me like one can only imagine. The blast of the shotgun missed me. What I felt was the percussion from the blast when it billowed out my pants. How it missed me I will never know.

Everything had calmed down. We were outside of the apartment house. I went up to the officer who was carrying the shotgun. I said, "Why the hell did you have your finger on the trigger when we entered the apartment? Your finger should have been on the outside of the trigger guard."

He looked at me, and I could see he was just as scared as I was when I thought I had been hit. He said, "D.H., I'm sorry. I had no idea my finger was on the trigger. I tripped on the rug in the hall."

I smiled and said, "Forget about it. It was only my ass anyhow."

The lieutenant assigned some guys to take the prisoners downtown to Central Booking. He turned to me and said, "Herlihy! Meet me at Ryan's Bar. I think you need a drink."

I replied, "How right you are!"

CHAPTER TWENTY-THREE

The big brass at headquarters felt that there were too many drugs being sold in Harlem (Wow! What a surprise!). He rounded up a task force in Harlem to try and stop it. This task force would be called "Operation Drug Bust" (brilliant name!). It would consist of men from Narcotics in all five boroughs. They would conduct "Buy and Bust" operations in order to lock up as many street dealers as possible.

Sergeant McGovern would lead the Brooklyn South team. This team consisted of myself, Frankie Shields, Al Brough, Kiernen Sheehan, Jimmy O'Neil and Al Kennedy. Many arrests were being made. The prisoners were taken to the 28th Precinct. There they were booked and lodged until the next morning. They would then be transported to 100 Center Street for arraignment.

Sergeant McGovern, Frankie Shields and I had a department undercover car at our disposal. We were not allowed to take a department car out of the city limits. When the tour ended, we would drive the car to my mother's house in Bayside, and park the department car in her driveway. We would then proceed on our way home to Long Island in Frankie's car.

It was a Sunday evening, April 17, 1977, and about 11 p.m. We were on our way home. Frankie was driving, Jack McGovern was in the rear seat, and I was in the passenger seat, and we were on the Long Island Expressway approaching the area between Guinea Woods Road and Jericho Turnpike. We were in the right lane talking about the job, when an eighteen-wheel tractor-trailer passed us in the middle lane. He must have thought that he had cleared our car and swung the trailer back into the right lane. His right rear wheel bumped our left front fender, sending Frankie's car to the right and up an embankment. The driver of the trailer never knew he hit us. Frankie tried desperately to control the car. We came down the embankment and across the three lanes of traffic before slamming into a four-foot cement barrier separating the east from the west traffic. The car went up in the air and landed on its roof in the left lane.

At this time, cars were not equipped with seat belts. The three of us bounced around the car like rubber balls. I must have temporarily lost consciousness. When I woke up, Frankie was lying on top of me. Jack was still unconscious in the rear lying on the interior roof. I said to Frankie, with a little laughter, "Will you get the fuck off of me?" It was then I realized the car was upside down. Jack was regaining consciousness, and I could smell gasoline inside the car.

Two black men were kneeling on the pavement where the windshield used to be. They said to Frankie, "Give me your arms, and we will pull you out." Frankie complied and they pulled him out through the opening in the windshield. They placed Frankie on the grass and quickly returned for Jack and me.

As they knelt down to remove me, I said, "You guys aren't smoking are you? There is gas coming into the car."

The one man said, "Give me your arm."

I moved my left hand. The only part that moved was the part above my bicep. A pointed bone below my shoulder was protruding out of my shirt. That was all that would move. I said to the guy, "Holy shit! Will you look at this!" I moved it back and forth. There was no pain.

The man screamed, "Don't do that! Give me your other arm."

I said, "I can't. It's behind my back." He told me to try and put my legs out through the opening, which I was able to do. Both men took hold of a leg and dragged me across the three traffic lanes on my back. I noticed, while being dragged, that the motor of the car was lying in the middle lane. Traffic was at a complete standstill.

They retrieved Jack from the car. The three of us were lying on the grass. The two men said, "Are you guys cops?"

Frankie replied, "Yeah."

The good samaritan said, "Here comes the Nassau Police and the Fire Department so we'll be going."

We thanked them and saw the flashing lights coming in and out of traffic on the Expressway. I thought to myself, how did these good samaritans know we were cops? I was holding my broken left arm and could feel the handle of my gun, which was still in its holster on my left side.

I looked at Frankie and Jack and said, "Do you guys have your guns?"

Jack was still woozy but replied, "I've got mine."

Frankie was bleeding pretty bad from a large cut on his head but reached for his ankle holster. He said, "Mine is gone."

I laughed and said, "Well there goes your gun down the road with the good samaritans."

Frankie smiled and said, "God bless them." I hope they don't use it. Maybe they'll just keep it as a souvenir."

I said, "Oh great! Tell that to the Review Board when they fine you five days pay for failure to safeguard your weapon." Frankie laughed.

We were all in pretty good spirits, just thankful to be alive, as the police and ambulance attendants placed us in the ambulance. The medic had put some wires on my chest. I heard over the radio, "Take that patient forthwith to the nearest hospital."

I looked at the medic and said, "Is that meant for me?" He didn't answer, so I didn't push the issue.

We arrived at Syosset Hospital Emergency Room. I was lying on one gurney and Frankie was sitting on another one right next to me. Jack was lying on a third. While Frankie and I were talking, I moved my right arm up to my chest and felt for my rib cage. I looked at Frankie and said, "Wow. My chest feels like a gigantic bowl of Jell-O. I can't feel any rib bones." I turned and saw my wife and a few of my daughters standing there.

I heard a doctor ask the nurse, "What is his blood pressure?"

The nurse responded, "Sixty over ten."

The doctor yelled, "Get him upstairs —STAT!"

The nurse started to move my gurney. I looked at Frankie and said, "Frankie, come with me, something is happening. I don't feel good."

He said, "I can't. They won't let me."

With that, the nurse started to wheel me hurriedly down a long hallway. A short distance down the hall, I could see a wall of pitch-black darkness. I was screaming at the nurse, "Don't wheel me into that darkness! PLEASE!" She couldn't hear me. There were no words coming out of my mouth. I couldn't move. Doesn't she see the darkness? The gurney was moving as if in slow motion. The darkness crept over my ankles that were under the sheet, and slowly to my knees. I once again screamed with no sound coming out of my mouth, "Nurse, Don't let the darkness go over my shoulders." She couldn't hear me. My eyes were wide open in a state of panic. "Nurse,- please, don't let the darkness go over my head." Once again, she couldn't hear me. The darkness was creeping over my chest. Just then, my whole body became engulfed in a black hole of horrible pitch-black darkness. A darkness that I never had experienced before in my life.

THE LIGHT! I didn't see a light. I felt it. My eyes were closed, and I could feel a light going through my whole body. I was in fear of opening my eyes. Finally, I did. This was the brightest light I have ever seen. There was nothing to the sides of the light or beyond the light. The light seemed to take up all the space. I closed my eyes ever so slowly. There were no thoughts of any kind in my mind except for that light. Time did not exist, not the day nor the month. It was as if I was suspended in some sort of space that wasn't there. Yet, that was the only thing that I was aware of, the space.

Time passed. How much, I had no idea. I opened my eyes, and there was a nurse standing with her back to me. My hands were tied down to the gurney. I was choking. Something was in my mouth, and I was choking. I made a grunting sound, and the nurse turned around. "Ah, you're awake!" I moved my fingers because I couldn't talk. The nurse looked at me and said, "Do you want to write something?"

I blinked frantically as if to say "yes." She untied my right hand and put a pen in it. She held a clipboard in front of me. I wrote "flem" and pointed to my throat.

She smiled and said, "Oh, you spelled the word wrong. It's p-h-l-e-g-m."

I looked at her as if she were crazy and thought to myself, "What am I in a spelling bee?"

I could see a machine, beside the nurse, with bellows going up and down. When the bellows went up, my chest went down. When the bellows went down, my chest would go up. I couldn't comprehend why the movement of the bellows would be making my chest move. I thought maybe it was just a coincidence.

The nurse turned her back towards me to get something from a tray. I reached up and grabbed ahold of this tube that was in my mouth. I pulled it out about four inches. It wouldn't all come out. I pulled even harder until I was able to get the whole tube out of my throat. Bells and low-sounding sirens screeched. All of a sudden, I couldn't breathe. I tried to take a deep breath, but I couldn't. It dawned on me that this tube was helping me breathe. I took hold of the tip of the tube and tried sucking some precious air. Nothing happened. I was getting dizzy.

Doctors and nurses started running into the room. The doctor grabbed an oxygen mask and forced oxygen into my lungs. He asked the nurse, "How did his hand become untied?"

She explained the situation to him. He looked at me and said, "You were not supposed to wake-up with the respirator still on you. But you did. The tube had a balloon on the end of it. I hope you didn't damage your larynx when you pulled it out. If you can stay awake and breathe like you are doing now for fifteen minutes with the forced oxygen, I won't put the tube back down your throat."

I said, "No tube. I'll stay awake." I glanced at a clock on the wall and waited for the minutes to tick by. Twenty minutes had passed. I thought, where the hell is he?

The door opened and the doctor came in. "You're still awake, good. I'll leave you on that machine." Out he went. Thank God I stayed awake. Now I can close my eyes for another long sleep.

The same nurse was there when I woke up. I asked her the time. "Three in the morning," she said. I asked her how long I had been here. She said, "You were in a very bad car accident yesterday." I told her that I remembered the accident. She said, "You're in an Intensive Care Unit now. When you were moved out of the Emergency Room, they lost you for two and a half minutes."

I said, "I don't understand."

She continued, "You stopped breathing for two and a half minutes. We brought you back." I looked at her trying to put everything in prospective.

She said, "You're a policeman and your wife is a registered nurse, right?"

I said, "Yes."

She looked at me and said, "I'm only telling you this because you are a cop and your wife is a nurse. I don't think this hospital can keep you alive. Your injuries are far more serious than you are being told. Your wife works in Mid-Island Hospital. If I were your wife, I would move you over there."

I starred at her. She could see the gratitude in my eyes. I said, "Would you call her right now and explain this to her?" She picked up the phone and called Carol. I heard her explain to her what she had told me. She then handed me the phone.

Carol spoke with a panic in her voice, "Don, what should I do?"

I said, "Call Patty Burns. He'll know what to do." I handed the phone back to the nurse and thanked her.

It was early morning when I heard Carol and Patty Burns arguing with a doctor. Patty was saying, "He is one of my cops and we are moving him."

The doctor said, "He has a broken rib near his heart. If you move him, the point of the rib could puncture his heart and it will kill him." Patty looked at Carol. She nodded, "yes."

Patty said to the doctor, "Give his wife the release and she will sign it. We will move him without making a wrinkle in the sheet."

Patty and Carol came to my side and said, "D.H., we are going to take you to Mid-Island Hospital in a police department ambulance. It is very important that you do not move a muscle." Two New York City Emergency Service officers brought a machine that slipped under the sheet that I was lying on. It lifted me up. Not a wrinkle in the sheet moved.

The ambulance driver drove about six miles an hour the seven miles to Mid-Island Hospital. The ride felt as if I were on an air-bed. Once again, I was put in the intensive care unit. Patty Burns pulled off the impossible again, as he always did. I was safe for the time being.

CHAPTER TWENTY-FOUR

A doctor entered my room. He introduced himself as Dr. Aleman, a chest surgeon. He said, "I'm a very good friend of your wife. She asked me to take good care of you." I nodded in agreement. He said, "I have to tell you about your injuries. Your head is cracked in five different places. Your left lung has collapsed. You have a flared chest, which means all of your ribs in the front and back are broken. You have chips of bone from your spine floating around in your back. Your spleen is dripping blood and could explode at any moment. You have a compound fracture of your left arm, and your lungs are filling up with fluid." He added with a smile, "Other than that, you are doing fine!" I smiled back at him.

He looked at me and said, "Do you have any questions for me?"

I replied, "I was told that they lost me for two and a half minutes. Does that mean I will have some brain damage, other than what I had before the accident?"

He said, "No. There should not be any damage. You would have to be gone for around five to six minutes for brain damage to occur. I am going to order a scan just to be on the safe side and for your peace of mind. I'm going to set your arm and put a cast on it right now." After my arm was put in a cast he said, "I have to put a hole in your back while you're awake so as to remove the fluid from your lungs. You will feel a pop when I enter your lung." And what a pop it was! It almost sent me out of the bed. I watched the fluid fill up what looked like a wine decanter.

I was in the hospital about three weeks. Carol, my children and Frankie were there constantly. One afternoon Dr. Aleman came in my room and asked me how I was doing. I told him that I must have slept on my cast, because I had a terrible pain on my right side. He looked at me and said, "Think about what you just said. You couldn't possibly have slept on your cast, which is on your left arm, and have a pain on your right side." He looked in my eyes, looked at my fingernails, and pressed his hand on my right side. I flinched! He yelled for a nurse.

I said, "What's wrong?"

He said, "Your spleen has ruptured, and you are bleeding internally. I only have about twenty minutes to operate on you or you will die."

I said, "You're shitting me, right? Are you telling me that you are going to cut my stomach open?"

He replied, "Yes!" He left the room. With that, the nurse put a paper hat of some kind on my head and began wheeling the bed to the operating room.

Dr. Aleman was already there in an operating gown. A nurse took my arm, the one in the cast, and was strapping it to a pole when I heard a loud click. I said, "Nurse, I think you just broke my arm again."

She said, "We have to operate on you immediately. Your arm is not important now. We'll worry about that later."

Someone put a mask over my face and said, "Goodnight." Once again, I was off to oblivion.

I woke up in the intensive care unit. All I kept thinking was when will this nightmare end. I noticed Carol, my kids, Frankie, and his wife, Susan, all standing by my bed. All of them had a worried look on their faces. I smiled and said, "I'm still here." About five days later, I was put back in a room on a regular floor.

Dr. Aleman came in to see me. I said, "I just remembered that when the nurse strapped my arm to the pole I heard a click."

He looked at me and said, "You should have told me this earlier." An x-ray was taken. The bone was already adhered to the broken part of my arm. It was too late to correct it. I would have somewhat of a golf ball of bone on my bicep. This would make my left arm stronger than my right arm. The bad news was that my left arm would be about one inch shorter than my right.

I said, "No sweat. I still have both my arms." I thought to myself, what the hell. I'm alive. There was a time when I thought they wouldn't have enough super glue to put me back together again.

I spent two and a half months in the hospital before I was released. I went home on a beautiful summer day, thanking God for my blessings and my life. My recovery would be long, but I was determined to become the same strong person that I was before the accident. Frankie would come over the house and keep me up-to-date on the Bulldog case.

Frankie explained to me that Lieutenant Walsh had decided to arrest Bulldog, hoping he would flip on his people. They arrested him as he left his home. Two of our detectives dressed in uniforms pulled his car over telling him that he went through a stop sign. Bulldog was not afraid of officers in uniform, only plainclothes cops. When he was asked to get out of the car, the officers pulled their guns and informed him that he was under arrest.

He replied, "You guys aren't real cops. You're from a unit!" They explained to him that he was under arrest for the sale of narcotics and read him his rights. While searching his car, they recovered two guns under the front seat. They asked Bulldog if he would have used the guns if he knew they were from the Narcotics Unit. He smiled and said, "I really don't know."

A search of his house, where his seventy-two year old mother lived, produced two kilos of heroin. They knew the drugs did not belong to the mother, so she was not arrested for possession. Bulldog was in deep shit and he knew it. What the lieutenant and the detectives on the case did not know was that Bulldog had no intention of giving up anyone. He would never flip. His oath to the "Family" meant more to him that any prison term he faced.

The officers on the case went into court with two years of hard evidence. The evidence included volumes of tapes, documents of buys, and the most damaging, testimony by Neil, the undercover that Bulldog trusted wholeheartedly. They even arrested a top Capo on a conspiracy charge that was given to the Federal Government. It was a well-known fact that New York City courts did not have a good batting average when it came to convictions on conspiracy cases. The Feds prosecuted the case against the Capo, and he received five years in a federal prison.

Bulldog's "Family" was not the kind to tolerate this kind of a mistake, especially one where he was hanging out with an undercover cop. Retaliation was sure to come. If not to him, it would certainly be against Bulldog's immediate family. As much as to say, "what goes around comes around."

Bulldog was sentenced to two life term prison sentences. They were to run consecutively. This meant he would never leave the prison alive. While in court, he approached Detective Pagnellie and asked to shake his hand. While reaching for his hand he said, "The name of the game was that I stay away from being caught. Your job was to see if you could catch me. The best man won." That said, Pagnellie very cautiously shook his hand. He went on to ask Pagnellie if he would watch out for his "Mudda and the dog," which was a miniature white poodle. "Just keep an eye on them," he asked. Pagnellie nodded his head in agreement.

Bulldog was serving his time in Sing Sing Prison, when the officers of Brooklyn South were asked to make an ID of a female found DOA on the Belt Parkway. Detective Pagnellie and Lieutenant Walsh responded to the location. There she was, Cleo, Bulldog's wife lying on the grass. She had two bullet holes in the back of her head from a .25 caliber pistol. This was an obvious sign from the revengeful "Family" for a payback to a soldier who was careless in his work.

A few days later, Lieutenant Walsh and Detective Pagnellie drove up to Sing Sing Prison to inform Bulldog what had happened to his wife. Retaliation had begun. Walsh and Pagnellie had hoped that Bulldog would be furious enough to turn and give up everyone in the "Family." When they informed Bulldog of his loss he said, "How's my Mudda and my dog?"

145

Detective Pagnellie looked at Walsh and then at Bulldog. "They're fine! I saw your mother on Flatbush Avenue the other day. She was walking the dog."

Bulldog turned to Pagnellie and said, "Thanks for driving up and telling me. Guard, the gate." He was finished talking and was going back to his cell.

About two or three months later, the office was notified by the New Jersey Police that Bulldog's eighteen-year-old son was thrown from a six story window to his death. Lieutenant Walsh and Detective Pagnellie once again drove the long ride up to Sing Sing Prison to inform Bulldog of the tragic loss of his son. Bulldog took the news very hard. Even Pagnellie and Walsh felt sorry for him. He starred at them and again asked, "How's my Mudda? How's my dog?"

The reply, "They're fine."

Bulldog turned and said, "Thanks. Guard, the gate."

Lieutenant Walsh and Detective Pagnellie were on the thruway heading back to the office. Walsh yelled out, "Son of a bitch!"

Pagnellie was startled and looked at Walsh, "What?"

Walsh replied, "We should have shot the God damn dog. If we had he would have given up Carlo Gambino himself." They both laughed, knowing that the payback from the "Family" towards Bulldog was over. And so was their case.

CHAPTER TWENTY-FIVE

You're fit for full duty! Those beautiful words were spoken to me by the police surgeon. It had taken me a full year to recuperate, and now I was as good as new. The anticipation of going back to work and seeing the guys was something I had been looking forward to for a long time. I could hardly believe that this day had finally arrived.

As I walked into the office, everyone started cheering and patting me on the back. I was truly in my glory. Lieutenant Walsh and Sergeant Jack McGovern came up to me and said, "Let's have a bite to eat at Ryan's." Nothing had changed. We had lunch and a couple of drinks. Afterwards, I accompanied Frankie, Al Brough and Jimmy O'Neil back to the office. It was time to get back in the saddle again.

A few months went by and I had information on a guy who was selling ounces of cocaine. We had to use an undercover that we hadn't used before in our work. All our regular undercover officers were working on cases for other teams. This undercover, who I will call "Abe," made a phone call to a subject. We were going to buy an ounce of cocaine. The undercover returned to us and said, "He wants three grand for the ounce." I looked at him and said, "What is he shitting us? For three grand he would have to give us eighty to eighty-two percent pure." The undercover shrugged his shoulders.

I looked at the lieutenant. He said, "If we can get pure and you verify it, then let's give it a shot."

The undercover set up the time and place for the buy. I went to One Police Plaza to get the buy money and record the serial numbers. When I returned, we were on our way. Lieutenant Walsh instructed Abe to meet up with us after the buy at a predetermined location. After the buy went down, Al Brough, Jimmy O'Neil and myself waited for Abe to appear out of the building. We followed him to the meeting place where Lieutenant Walsh was waiting.

Al Brough went to the police lab with Abe. The rest of the team went back to the office. A lab report containing the "Q and Q," quality and quantity, would not be available to us for a few days. In the meantime, we worked on other cases. When we received the lab report, it was not the pure cocaine as we expected. It was around forty-two percent. The lieutenant was livid about us spending that kind of money on a buy when we weren't sure of the quality. We received a good ass chewing. He explained that we should have gotten a taste, which is a small amount of cocaine, before committing ourselves. We would have been able to test it before making a large buy. We all knew that he was right. With our experience, we should have known better. You can bet your life that he had some explaining to do to the higher brass downtown.

We all got together with Lieutenant Walsh and said that we were going to pick up this mutt. It wouldn't matter if we burned the undercover, because we would not be buying from the subject again. We went to the apartment and arrested the subject. I said to him, "You have balls selling garbage like that for three grand."

He looked at us as if we were crazy. He said, "Three grand! I sold that guy an ounce for fifteen hundred. What the hell are you talking about three grand?"

I looked at Al Brough and Jimmy O'Neil and said, "Shit, we got trouble. We have to call Walsh right away, and explain this to him."

The lieutenant met with us and listened to every word of the subject's story. He called us over to the side and said, "I think we have a dirty undercover detective. I'm going to notify IAD." All the proper notifications were made. We met with the people from IAD. As much as we hated this, it was something that had to be done.

Internal Affairs told us to call Abe and tell him that we were going to try another buy on the subject, hoping we would be able to get our hands on some pure stuff. Undercover officers know how narcotics detectives work. They will make a few buys over a period of time. They will leave the subject out there for a period of months. This was to ensure that the identity of the undercover, or time and place of the buy, would not be remembered by the subject. It was our thought that Abe was counting on having that window of opportunity, so he could deny any allegations brought against him three or six months down the road by the subject on the buy.

IAD told the subject that he must do exactly as they say. In return, they will contemplate dropping his first sale of narcotics, providing he is telling the truth. He was told to accept the call from Abe and go through the same motions as he did on the first sale. We contacted Abe at the undercover office. We told him to meet us in the Brooklyn South Office so we can set up another buy for an ounce from the same subject. We also mentioned to him that maybe we would get lucky this time and get some good quality coke for a change.

Abe met with us and made the call to the subject. He told us everything was a "Go" for three thousand dollars again. The buy money was already in our hands and the serial numbers recorded. We headed to the location of the buy. After the buy went down, Al Brough and I followed the undercover to a meeting place where Lieutenant Walsh and IAD were waiting. Detectives Jimmy O'Neil and Kiernan Sheehan would bring the subject of the buy, minutes later, to the same meet.

Undercover Abe said, "Everything went great. Who will be coming with me to the lab?" Although he saw two extra detectives with Walsh, he assumed they were from Brooklyn South narcotics. When the subject appeared on the scene minutes later, Abe's expression totally changed. He said, "What's going on?"

The Lieutenant from IAD looked at O'Neil and Sheehan as he asked the subject "How much was that buy?"

The subject replied, "Fifteen hundred." Detective Jimmy O'Neil turned over the fifteen hundred from the subject to the lieutenant from IAD.

IAD immediately searched Abe. They removed his weapon, shield and fifteen hundred in cash. The serial numbers matched with the recorded buy money. Abe was placed under arrest and went off with IAD. As we drove back to the office, I said to Frankie, "I will never understand what makes a cop think that he can outsmart his fellow cops. Why wouldn't he think that we would be pissed off enough to go back and arrest the subject when he didn't deliver what he promised?"

Frankie said, "He took a shot. Knowing we leave people out there for a while, he thought we would do a second buy a few weeks from now. The more time between buys, the more credible his story would be." Frankie continued, "He would say, 'hat junkie dealer charged three grand both times. Now, who are you going to believe him or me?' Time would have been on his side."

I said, "Well he's going to have a lot of time on his side now!"

We met the guys at Ryan's Bar, as usual, and had a couple of drinks. We watched Frankie belly up to the shuffleboard and yell out, "Alright. Herlihy and I have the next challenge." I thought to myself, things don't change, they just get better.

A year has passed. I have about nineteen years on the force. I am still in narcotics setting up buys. In my spare time, I try to beat Frankie at that damn shuffleboard game. I have spent the last six years in narcotics, and our team has become quite proficient at doing our job.

CHAPTER TWENTY-SIX

Lieutenant Walsh was asked if he would fill in at Manhattan South Narcotics office. This office was located in the Seventh Precinct, located alongside of the Manhattan Bridge. They picked Lieutenant Walsh because of his outstanding work in Brooklyn South Narcotics. The assignment was supposed to be temporary. However, much to the dismay of Lieutenant Walsh, it eventually became a permanent move.

Sergeant McGovern, along with the rest of the team, felt lost without Lieutenant Walsh as our commander. The news that Walsh would not be returning was devastating to all of us in the Tenth Narcotics Division.

A few weeks later, I received a phone call from Walsh. He asked me if I would consider transferring to Manhattan South Unit to build some cases for him. I thought for a minute and said, "Alright. I'll put in a U.F. 57. Just make sure that I get transferred to you and not somewhere like Elephant Breath Montana.

He said, "Just put the paperwork in and I will pick you up."

I wasn't overjoyed about leaving the guys in Brooklyn South. Walsh and I had become close over time, and I liked working with him ever since we met many years ago while in uniform. About a week later, I walked into the office of Manhattan South and was introduced to my new team.

Manhattan South Narcotics was a busy office. It comprised the Fifth and the Ninth Precincts. These areas were drug havens beyond belief. Eldridge Street, near Stanton Street on the lower east side of Manhattan, was damn near a fortress in itself. There were so many lookouts on the street. Whenever a car that was suspected to be a police car went by, the whistles could be heard a block away. Kids nine and ten years old were being paid to be lookouts. We couldn't walk down a block without hearing a whistle alarm going out.

We had made many buys in the block with undercover officers, but going in the block to make arrests of the subjects was almost impossible. By the time we got to our destination, the subjects were in the wind. The well-known whistles would be a warning that the "Man" was in the block.

We had spent numerous hours observing the street. I had noticed that whenever a rental vehicle like Avis or a Ryder truck went through the street, no whistles were heard. I suggested to Lieutenant Walsh that we rent two or three Avis trucks and put twenty or so men in the back of the trucks. We would be able to enter the block without the lookouts giving us a second glance. This would enable us to stop at the buildings of our choice, and the men could jump out the back of the truck and do their thing.

Lieutenant Walsh liked the idea and set the plans in motion. He had the tasks of renting the trucks and obtaining the numerous search warrants on the tenements where the undercovers had bought drugs. He massed together about one hundred and thirty officers to hit five tenements on the block simultaneously. Every officer had his orders as to which building and apartment he was to hit. They were informed how the apartments were laid out and on what floor each apartment was located.

The day arrived. It was a cold day on February 8, 1980. Four trucks with the name "Avis" boldly written on the side entered the forbidden street. The trucks came to an abrupt stop in front of their designated tenements. The rear sliding doors of every truck were flung open. More than one hundred cops leaped out of the trucks, which were loaded with shotguns, battering rams, rifles, and handguns. Every cop wore a full metal bulletproof jacket vest. The civilians in the area must have thought they were being invaded by a war. It was, in fact, a war that the New York Police Department had long ago declared on drugs.

It was a miracle that no shots were fired. They were taken completely by surprise. If the thought had crossed any of the perpetrator's minds to have a shoot out, they didn't act on that thought. They knew that they would most definitely be killed if they lifted a weapon. They were out-numbered by both cops and weapons.

The next day, the following report appeared in the Daily News:

"RAIDERS KNOCK OUT DRUG SUPERMARKET"

A small army of 130 police officers, armed with rifles and shotguns, burst into five tenements on Eldridge Street on the lower East Side yesterday to break up what they said was a well organized collection of drug factories and retail "supermarkets." It was the largest bust ever in the entire tri-state area. The raiders collared sixty people and seized pills, heroin, cocaine, marijuana, and a bundle of cash and weapons. Police said the buildings were protected by vicious dogs and armed guards. They said two weeks ago they videotaped 300 to 400 people an hour visiting to make drug purchases. The operation grossed $1 million a week.

The paper carried pictures of the actual bust and the officers involved. There were pictures taken in the station house of wall-to-wall prisoners that were arrested. I felt very proud to be among the men that carried out this flawless operation.

The next week, it was back to work on our other cases. This one case in particular involved a nineteen-year-old boy. The undercover, who had made three or four buys from him, nicknamed him "John Doe Gun." The reason for this name was due to the fact that we were unable to obtain a positive identification on him. Whenever the undercover made a buy, the subject made it a point to let the undercover see a gun in his belt. The team called him a "wanna be gangster kid."

Without a positive ID, this kid could be in the wind at any time. It was time to pick him up. The plans were set. Lieutenant Walsh and myself would knock on the door of his apartment. Officers from our team would cover the fire escape in the rear. When he would open the door, we would inform him that he was under arrest for the sale of narcotics. I don't know if age becomes a factor as time goes by, or we just become careless. I think a better word might be that we become too "relaxed" at what we are doing. We start to take things for granted. When this happens, it could cost us our life. This arrest would be just that type of situation.

Lieutenant Walsh and I were talking as we knocked on the door of the subject's apartment. We announced, "Police!" I heard the shot as the bullet passed through the wooden door between our heads. We immediately jumped to either side of the door pressing our backs against the wall while drawing our weapons at the same time. This is the position we should have been in when we first knocked on the door. It is one of the most basic rules taught to every rookie in the Police Academy.

At any rate, we heard the team in the rear announce over the radio, "We have the subject in custody. We caught him coming down the fire escape. Is everyone alright up there?" The Lieutenant kicked the door open. We entered a one bedroom apartment with no one else in it. As we looked out the open window, we saw the team leading the subject to the street and signaled them that we were okay.

We closed the door to the apartment and stood looking at the bullet hole in the door. Neither one of us spoke. We knew that we had fucked up by standing in front of the door. The bullet had passed inches from either side of our heads. Six inches to the left, and it would have hit me in the face. Six inches to the right would have caught Walsh in the face. We met the team in the street. They showed us the nine millimeter gun the kid had fired. Walsh nodded. The team took the subject to Central Booking. I looked at Walsh and said, "I need a fucking drink!"

Walsh looked at me and said, "I know a nice little pub in the Fifties, let's go!"

We sat at the bar. I was looking at Walsh in the mirror behind the bar. I said, "I think I'm going to pack it in." Jerry didn't answer at first. He was starring at his drink.

He said, "What are you talking about?"

I said, "You know! I'm going to put my papers in and retire. I feel that the handwriting is on the wall. There's a bullet out there with my name on it. If you think about it, I'm forty-five years old and your forty-three, and here we are playing a young man's dangerous game."

Jerry smiled and said, "You could be right about that."

I said, "I don't want my family attending a bullshit inspector's funeral. I lived through the Korean War, fourteen years in uniform, and seven years in Narcotics. I think it's time."

I knew that Jerry wasn't expecting this. He said, "What will you do out there?"

I smiled and said, "I'll be alive to sign my retirement papers, that's what I'll do." Jerry started laughing as he told the bartender to pour us another round.

A few weeks later, I put in for a temporary assignment to Queens Homicide to wait out my few weeks before retiring. It was approved. I reported to the 112th Precinct, which housed the Homicide Squad. I would do some time on desk duty until I was ready to make the final move.

The day arrived. I decided to go to Headquarters and finalize my papers for retirement. It was a sad task for me but one that I knew in my heart had to be done. I was standing in line waiting for my turn at the window to turn in my shield. I handed the officer behind the window my papers and police shield #5254. He took the paperwork and shield. He tossed my shield on a pile of other shields, as if it were garbage and said, "Next."

I stood there starring at him and said, "I carried that shield for twenty-one years and you toss it like it was a piece of shit. Give me back my shield!" He looked at me as if I were crazy as he handed me back the shield. I took it back and said to him, "Now,

Officer, will you please place my shield gently on that table?" He had a frightened look on his face but did as I asked.

Behind me I heard, "What the hell is the holdup?"

I knew that voice. I turned around and there he was, Jerry Walsh, handing in his shield for retirement. I smiled and said, "I didn't know you were going to retire?"

He said, "Hell, you were right. It's a young man's game out there."

After we signed a few thousand papers, we went across the street to the Metropolitan Pub. It was a very hot day in August of 1981 as we toasted each other on our retirement. There was no one else around. We celebrated by ourselves for hours.

A few weeks later my friends and family threw a retirement party for Jerry and myself. It was held in a restaurant called The Assembly located in Bayside. Guys from the Nineteenth Precinct, Brooklyn South Narcotics, and friends that Jerry and I had made over the years were there. Frankie Shields was in charge of announcing everyone. You can imagine the laughs that we had with him. A good time was had by all.

Mama was smiling from ear to ear. Her Donald had made her dream come true. He put in twenty-one years in the New York City Police Department and now would have a pension for the rest of his life. Just like Mama said, Donald made her proud.

My father died in 1979. I lost Mama in 1982. They both had lived a full and happy life. When I lost my mother, I lost my best friend. Mama was the only one that I would confide in if I had a problem.

On November 16, 1982, twelve days after the loss of my mother, my wife Carol approached me as I was lying on the couch nursing a hangover. She said, "Don, I think it would be best for the kids if you moved out." I just looked at her as she went on to say, "I can't put up with your constant drinking and coming home drunk all the time." I didn't say a word. She said, "I'm going to King Kullen Supermarket now."

I stood up and said, "That's it? You're throwing me out in the street. I just want you to know—I will survive!"

Carol left the house. I went into the bedroom and packed two suitcases with all my clothes. As I put the suitcases in the trunk of the car, I started laughing. I thought to myself, after twenty-four years of marriage, all I own fits in two suitcases. I made a call to a buddy of mine, Jim Cartwright. He was a Suffolk County Police Officer. I asked him if he could put me up for awhile until I found a place of my own. He said, "Hell yeah! It's just me alone in this big house. Come on over." Jim was also divorced. We had become good drinking buddies over the years. We partied for what seemed like forever. We hit just about every bar from Long Island to Atlantic City to Las Vegas. I stayed with Jim for about six months. I found a nice furnished apartment in Deer Park, Long Island.

CHAPTER TWENTY-SEVEN

For the next twelve years, I would lead a very happy single life. My kids kept in contact with me. I would either hear from them or they would stop over my apartment at least once a week.

My oldest daughter, Debbie, works for ABC Television and has a very prestigious job. She is dating a nice guy by the name of Scott. My daughter, Carolyn, married Teddy. Teddy is a New York City Police Officer. They blessed me with two beautiful grandchildren, Matthew and Jaclyn. Colleen, my third daughter, is a paralegal with a law firm and married Scottie. Scottie, also a very nice guy, has two sons, Jason and Cory. Colleen enjoys helping Scottie with the children and raises them as if they were her own. My son, Donald, has his own carpentry business on Long Island building decks. He married Denise and they too blessed me with two beautiful grandchildren, Ryan and Ashley. Then there is my baby, Cathleen. As time went by, she met a very nice guy by the name of Jim. Jim owns and operates an Italian restaurant in the town of Huntington.

Now and then I would work with Donald on carpentry jobs building decks. We made a good team. I had taught him the trade when he was sixteen. Donald studied the trade in high school his last two years. He excelled in this trade and now is an accomplished carpenter. Whenever I worked with him, I would casually mention that I would like it if he became a New York City Police Officer. His answer to me was, "Dad, I hate cops. Why would I want to give up my business to be a cop?"

I said, "In twenty years, you could have a pension. Why don't you give it some thought? You would make your dad very proud." It felt like déjà vu all over again. The only difference was a father talking to his son.

Years were flying by at a very fast rate. Cartwright and myself were drinking our ass off to our heart's content. Jim and I would frequently meet at a bar and restaurant across from his house. We would have a couple of drinks and a bite to eat. This one particular night the waitress came over to take our order. Jim introduced me to her as Connie. At first glance, I thought to myself, God, she's beautiful. She had a great fun-loving personality.

Jim saw me looking at her and said, "Forget it. She's married."

I smiled and said, "That's true of all the nice ones." Jim was dating the bartender, Darlene. We frequented the place often so he could see her.

I tracked down my friend, Jerry Beckerman, and would drive out to the Hamptons to see him and his wife, Phyllis. Our other friend, Stewie, had been killed in a car accident a few years earlier. We would bullshit for awhile and then head out to Brooklyn to see Don Hart.

D.H. was still on the job. I told him he was crazy for staying because he was putting his pension at risk. I told him that it would only take one screw-up for them to take the pension away. He would be left with nothing after putting in all those years. Don Hart disagreed. It was eight years later that D.H. would feel the brunt of what I had said.

Don Hart was working in a detective unit that was keeping tabs on building inspectors. The story was that D.H. had a white department van that was used for stakeouts. One day he was in the Motor Pool and saw four tires that he could use on the van. The tires presently on the van were pretty worn. He told the guy that was on duty at the time, "Throw those tires in my van. While you're at it, I'll take the police radio, too."

About one month later, he was called down to IAD to be investigated for stealing department property. They assumed that the white van was Don Hart's private vehicle. This is how lax they were in so many of their investigations. D.H. told them that the white van was a police department vehicle, and the tires they were accusing him of stealing are on that van along with the radio, which is connected to the dashboard. After that incident, D.H. got the message and packed it in after twenty-nine years on the job.

It was the winter of 1988 when I decided that I had enough of the snow and cold weather. I again packed those two lonely suitcases and set out for sunny Florida. I called my cousin, Richie, and his wife, Jeanne, and asked them to find a furnished apartment for me. I stayed with Richie and Jeanne for about two weeks and then moved into a beautiful apartment.

Florida was where I belonged—with the beach, the sand, and the surf. I was in my glory and loved the life of a beach bum. The beach bars were plentiful, and I knew them all. Now and then I would have dinner at Richie and Jeanne's house. I knew that someday I would have to go back to New York to see my family. My lease was up in the winter of 1989. I had been living in Florida for a little over a year. This would be a good time to head back to New York and to see if I would miss Florida.

I again stayed at Jim Cartwright's house for a few weeks until I found an apartment. The holidays were getting close. I decided to get some Christmas shopping done before it was too late. As I was walking in the mall, I couldn't believe my eyes. There she was, Connie, the waitress from the bar and restaurant. She was selling massage pillows with another girl. The other girl turned out to be her sister, Marie. Connie explained to me that she was going through a divorce. I told her how sorry I was but, unbeknownst to her, I couldn't have been happier.

I asked Connie out that weekend and she agreed. As time went by, we became a steady item. I fell madly in love with her, as she did with me. We had been seeing each other for about two years. I was living in an apartment and my lease was about to end. Connie suggested that I move into her house with her two teenage children, Stephen and Debra. I told her that I would agree but her kids would have to approve. Connie explained to her kids that we were very much in love and were contemplating marriage in the future. The kids went along with the idea. I wasn't too sure how it would work out. I knew how teenagers could think. They might see you as someone who could threaten their world. It didn't turn out to be that way at all. The kids welcomed me and made me feel very comfortable. Debra showed me respect, and Stephen turned out to be my future stepson, and my best friend.

In 1994, my son Donald became a New York City Police Officer. It was only then that I knew how proud Mama must have felt so many years ago. Two years later, both Connie and myself sold our homes. We combined the proceeds from each house to buy a home in Coral Springs, Florida. We were married on January 11, 1997. My dream of someday marrying this girl had come true. We were both getting a second chance at a beautiful life together. The minister pronounced us husband and wife in a small church ceremony in Coral Springs, Florida.

Shortly thereafter, our son Stephen met and married a very nice girl by the name of Carol. They blessed us with our granddaughter, Julianna. Our daughter, Debra, met and married her longtime friend, Frank. They made the perfect couple.

Our son, Donald, was promoted to detective in the year 2000. He was transferred to the Queens Warrant Squad and is still. Donald often calls me and says, "You know, Dad, I only have ten more years before I can retire. I'm glad you made me become a cop."

I said to him, "Donald, it's obvious you love the job just as much as I did. You made this father very proud." In Donald's off duty time, he still works at the carpentry business for an extra income.

Connie and I live in a large waterfront home. All of our children, except Stephen and his family, still live in New York. Not a month goes by, when one of the kids aren't staying with us on a vacation. Connie and I are truly blessed with all our children and the love we have for each other.

We are frequently visited by our friends, Don and Joan Hart. A couple of times a year we also get together with Joe and Maryann Spinelli. Spinelli is Maryann's married name. I knew her when she was Maryann Messina, an undercover police officer in the

Narcotics Unit. She was a good undercover officer and Brooklyn South would use her on a few operations. Maryann was introduced to Joe by another policewoman friend of mine, Roslyn Lunetta. Lieutenant Walsh and his wife, Alma, moved to Texas, making the Lone Star State his home for retirement. We constantly keep in touch by phone.

Connie and I have seven beautiful children. We are very proud of all of them and their families. Carol and Stephen are expecting another child, a boy, which will make eight. As this book was being completed, my baby, who is now 33 years of age, Cathleen, and Jim arrived in Florida for a vacation. They sat us down and told us that we were going to be grandparents, again. This will bring the grandchild count to nine.

Life doesn't get any better than this...

Mama would be very, very proud!